THE TRUTH WILL DO

HOW TO GROW YOUR CHIROPRACTIC PRACTICE BY GETTING PATIENTS TO WANT WHAT THEY NEED

BY DR. DAVID JACKSON

#1 BESTSELLING AUTHOR

FREE COMMUNICATION TOOLS

Dig deeper with live video demonstrations of several of the communication tools taught in this book as well as real-life examples of the impact they create when implemented.

To further grow your practice by getting patients to WANT what they NEED, visit:

MYEPICPRACTICE.COM/TRUTH

CONTENTS

THIS BOOK IS DEDICATED TO THE
PEOPLE WE ARE CALLED TO SERVE.

FOR THEM, ONLY **THE TRUTH WILL DO**

1 THE TRUTH

"THE TRUTH IS INCONTROVERTIBLE. MALICE MAY ATTACK IT, IGNORANCE MAY DERIDE IT, BUT IN THE END, THERE IT IS."

-WINSTON CHURCHILL

We suck at communication.

I realize opening a book about communication with a harsh statement is abrupt, but our time is valuable and this is the single most important concept for us to grasp in chiropractic. We do suck at communication. Perhaps you're great at it. I've certainly worked hard to become great at it, but as a profession we are far from good at communicating the true benefits of chiropractic care.

Need proof? Look around.

The average chiropractor today graduates with between $175,000 - $200,000 in student loan debt, and that's not counting startup funds.

The average chiropractor sees less than 100 patient visits per week, meaning they actually serve 40, maybe, 50 individuals. Those individuals, on average, are seen between nine to twelve times in their lifetime. And the average chiropractor today brings home under $70,000 a year in personal income.

We have a problem. Ask anyone in the profession today and they'll say we've got a *lot* of problems.

I believe we have one: an inability to communicate perceived value to the people that matter most. In this book, I'm going to share an exact strategy of how to change that.

You know that saying "the truth hurts"? It does. I'm speaking from experience because it hurt me badly. How bad? Here is a little history:

Like many of you, I went to chiropractic school because my life was changed by it. I was involved in a bad automobile accident and tried everything to recover from it. After basically being told I'd have live with it, I found my way into a chiropractic office. My first adjustment was nothing short of a miracle. From that day on, I was committed to chiropractic. I was excited. I found a school and pushed myself through the BS of chemistry, physics and all of the other prerequisites. I went to LACC and graduated after four years with big hopes and two main goals:

1. **I wanted to help people**
2. **I wanted to make a decent living**

That was it. Very, very simple. Pretty hard to fall short of those simple, nebulous goals, but I didn't just miss them… I fell on my face. I failed. And I didn't fail once. I didn't fail twice.

I failed nine times.

I opened, operated, began and failed in nine different practices over the course of my first two and a half years after graduation. Now, I'm pretty resilient. I bounced back. I've never been a quitter my entire life, but I have to be honest with you. Two and a half years in, after almost eight years of study, borrowing $120,000, deferring that loan over two and a half years and living on nothing except the goodwill and grace of my mom, I'd had it.

I lost everything.

I don't mean money, because I didn't have any and I don't mean a house, because I lived at home in a basement. I mean I lost my belief in myself. I was down. For the first time in my life, I was truly distraught. I was depressed. The entire life vision I had built for myself came crashing down, and I will never forget the moment that it all happened.

When I was ten years old my father was diagnosed with terminal cancer. After lying sick in our living room on a hospital bed for three and a half years, he decided it was time to teach me some life lessons.

He sat down with me and told me something I remember vividly. He said, *David, always tell the truth. When you look someone in the eye, they'll know if you're telling the truth or not, and if you can't look them in the eye, then you're not going to be able to tell the truth.*

I didn't realize at the time just how much that would mean to me. Three years later, he passed away. He was 36. I was 13. I never thought about that lesson again until 1989.

It happened when I was sitting in front of Mary, explaining her report of findings and doing the best I could to tell her that I could help her with her migraines. I was going to present my care plan for her (and I say that with laughter in my heart, because it wasn't really a care plan at the time) which was that I'd work on her a couple of times and we'd see how it'd go.

Not the best of care plans, but it was the best I had at the time. I was about to tell her how much it was going to cost and since I took full insurance at the time, it was probably going to be $100 tops for her care. While I did my best to tell her I could help her, the time it would take, and the money it would cost, I couldn't look at her.

I couldn't look her in the eye.

I failed over and over and over again. On my biggest day in practice I only saw nine patients. I would be lucky to get three to five new patients per month, let alone have them last more than a visit or two. Yet, as I sat down with Mary, it all hit me. My dad's words came back to me. It was then I knew I was a fraud. I didn't believe. I was selling something that I didn't own.

I couldn't look at myself in the mirror.

Later that day when the office closed, I took my diploma off the wall and snapped the three-quarter inch walnut backing in half. I tore my diploma up, put it in a garbage can and lit it on fire.

One week later, I was under the hood of a car as an auto mechanic, never wanting to look back at this thing called chiropractic. I hated chiropractic. I hated that I wasted my life, my time and money that I would never get back. I wanted nothing to do with it ever again. I failed, and I quit.

Fast forward less than a year later: boy's friend sets him up on a blind date, boy doesn't want to on blind date, but boy's friend forces him to. Boy meets girl and falls in love. Boy tries to fight it but can't. Boy and girl are in two different states. Boy doesn't tell her his story or what he really does (he is a mechanic), so girl thinks boy is a doctor. Boy thinks, *it's okay, I'll never see her again,* then boy realizes, *oh my gosh, I'm going to marry her.* Five months later there's a date set. Boy panics and asks himself, *what am I going to do?* Boy says, *I better become a chiropractor again... quickly.*

Six months after I quit chiropractic and became an auto mechanic, I had to find another job... as a chiropractor. So I did. But this time something happened. I had a newfound purpose (love) and was simultaneously 'found' by a well-meaning and passionate chiropractor who, really against my will, pulled me up from my bootstraps and asked me, *what do you really want?* He told me his story. He shared his truth, something that I had never entertained before and somehow, I caught a glimpse of what mine could be like.

Now, I'm not suggesting it was easy, but within five months I was married and within six months my new wife (who is not a chiropractor) and I had started our own practice. We opened our practice and within a few months, we were serving over 100 patients a day. I went on to build a second practice that saw high volume, was 60% kids and accepted cash only. We were at a 65% profit margin and I was practicing 17 hours per week.

I had figured it out. It wasn't overnight, but I figured out what worked for me. In the years that followed Docs were constantly asking me how I did it, what changed. Sharing the answers took me around the world. I've spoken on five continents to over 10,000 chiropractors. I've coached and trained thousands of chiropractors through Epic Practice on how to master communication.

Through my experiences, I learned how to tell the truth. I learned how to be authentic. But most importantly, I learned how to get patients to share *their* truths. Once I learned their truths, I measured the gap- the distance between my truth and their truths- and mastered the art of communication to narrow the gap and deliver the results they deserve.

Man, I have to tell you something and Doc, you know this. The ability to look a man, woman or child in the eye and say, *here's what you need, here's what it's going to take, here's what we can deliver and here's what you can expect. Sign here. I've got a table with your name on it, waiting for you. I'm going to get you face down and change your life*- the difference between that feeling and the feeling I had each time I failed is worth the price of admission. It is true that the truth hurts, but it is also true that the truth shall set you free.

It all depends on where you stand.

2 THE ACTION

"THE RESULTS YOU HAVE ARE THE DIRECT EFFECT OF THE ACTIONS YOU TAKE. PERIOD."

-DR. DAVID JACKSON

It's been said that in order to have something you've never had, you have to do something you've never done. That that couldn't be closer to the truth when it comes to your ability to communicate, regardless if you're a startup or if you've been in practice 10 or 15 years.

We have all formed habits. Many of them become ruts. Some are okay, most are not, and you'll know by looking at the current result and overall status of your practice. If you have work to do, then let's do it.

There are three core areas that we need to look at and take action upon in order to fill the old ruts and build new pathways as we move towards a more congruent and authentic communication style that gives us what we actually want: the ability to serve the population and our own families without creating stress and burnout.

The first problem we're going to tackle in this book is our own chiropractic BS. It's easy to interpret BS and we all know there's a lot of it in this profession. I mean, where do we even begin?

But the BS I'm talking about goes well beyond the infighting and the division. Beyond the straights vs the mixers in schools, beyond insurance vs cash, beyond upper cervical vs tonal technique. We need to drop all of that BS... but that's not the BS I'm referring to.

The BS I'm talking about is our ***Belief System.***

It's the things we've been told, the things we accept as true, the things that drive the reasons we do what we do. It is those very belief systems that we MUST get past. We've got to look at them from a different angle and ask *if* and *how* they serve us. Once we do this, we can begin to take action.

The main strategy I'm going to help you understand and utilize in order to take action is a simple, yet profound tool I developed for myself some 15 years ago: The Epic BElief Triangle.

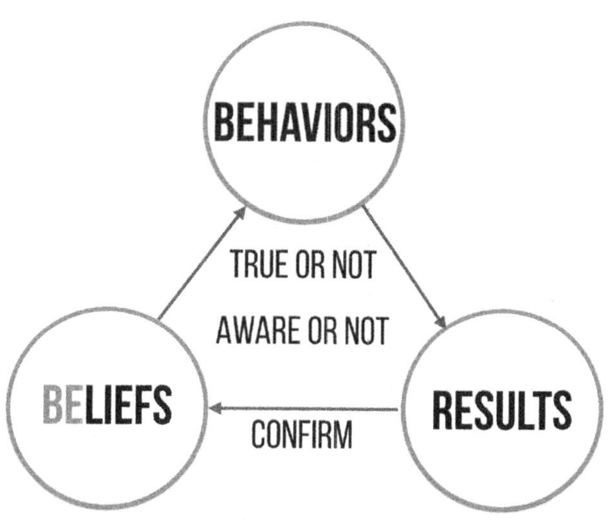

The Epic BElief Triangle is formed by three circles: one on the bottom left, one on the top, and one on the bottom right. Since we always begin with the end in mind, we're going to begin with the **Results** circle. When you want to take action, you must have a clear definition of what it is you are asking for and what you want the result to be. The results have to be clear, they have to be concise, and they have to be measurable. So we begin with the results.

What I'd like you to do now is get a blank piece of paper and draw a triangle. In the bottom right-hand corner, write down the **results** you have *right now.* Don't get carried away. Don't write everything down and don't limit it to just your chiropractic practice. Remember, results can be things you have that you want or things you have that you don't want, as well as things that you want to have that you currently don't.

It may mean, *I have $200,000 worth of student loans,* it may mean, *I'm collecting $16,000 per year* or a result may mean, *I average seven new patients per month* or, *I average 122 patient visits per week* or, *my PVA, my retention, my sick rate is twelve.* But what are the big ones, the KPIs (Key Performance Indicators)? What are THOSE when it comes to the results?

Let's move to the top of the triangle. In the top circle, you're going to see the word **BEhaviors**. You can also write in Actions or other similar words that mean these are the things causative to your results. These are what *create* the results. Every result you have is an effect from an action you took or did not take. Something you did or did not do.

For example, if you have a result of seven new patients per month and you're unhappy with it, write down the big rocks, the KPI in and around the word **BEhavior**. What did you do or not do? Did you do any Facebook lives? Have you been out doing workshops? Do you have a referral strategy in your office? Are you running at least one, if not two events per month? Do you have a 12 month marketing calendar? If you don't, it's not a shame, it's not a judgment, it's a fact.

Put it down as an action or inaction. If you have 110 patient visits per week, what are your actions? Put down whatever contributed to that positive or negative result, put down what actions or inactions you took. Are you calling your patients after their first visit? Are you asking them for referrals? These things are directly related to the KPI, to those big numbers you put down in the results.

So now we've got two-thirds of the triangle built. We have an active result *now,* so we're not talking about future pacing yet, and we have the actions that are contributing to those results.

This is where most people stop.

They say, *I just have to do things differently*. They say, *I've got to take more action* and they say *if I just learned this script* and so on. They think they need to go to another seminar so they can have another guru tell them how to do something, but it's not that we don't have enough to do. People do and do so much, that they end up right in a pile of do.

The problem is that as chiropractors, we should know better; regardless of where you went to school and regardless of how you practice. We as chiropractors understand better than almost any other profession the true law of cause and effect. We understand that behaviors, while they are contributory and causal to effects, are not a cause in and amongst themselves. Our behaviors and results are both effects of our beliefs. Those beliefs, whether you're conscious of them or not, whether they are truthful or not, compel you to action or inaction.

Every. Single. Time.

Yep, you heard me right. Whether you know you have a belief, or whether that belief is true or not, the reason you take action or do not take action is because of the belief systems that are instilled within you.

You have a poor result with your office visit average? Your care plans? You sit there and look at your actions and say, *well I don't really give people care plans because I don't know what to tell them.* Do you know why you've reacted this way? It's not because you don't know how to say, *hey Mary, it's going to take approximately 48 adjustments just to prepare you for life and wellness care.*

That's the script, but that's not the problem.

The problem is that there's a belief system inside you making you question yourself: *Is that what they need? How do I know it's going to help them? What if they start feeling better right away? What if they don't feel better on time? What if someone asks them why they keep going back? What if they think I'm after their money and that I don't care about their health? What if I don't spend enough time with them? What if I'm wrong? What if they don't like me? What if insurance won't pay?*

These belief systems drive our behaviors which dictate our results which then confirm those very belief systems.

For those of us climbing up and up towards success, it's an upward spiral because your results confirm that you have powerful, positive beliefs. Those on an upward spiral feel encouraged. *I'm going to do more Facebook Live. I'm going to do more workshops, that was freaking awesome, I had 17 moms show up and 22 new patients scheduled. I'm doing that again. We're going to take more action and get an even bigger result.* It confirms that belief was absolutely stellar, congruent and worked out beautifully.

On the other hand, if you have a half-assed belief you take half-assed action. You get less than a half-assed result and then it confirms: *I knew Dr. David was wrong, I knew that person was wrong. I've tried that before, it might work in their town, but it doesn't work in my town.*

Your beliefs drive your behaviors.

Whether they are true or not or whether you've identified them or not, they exist. The key to action is understanding that we have BS, or belief systems that drive our actions. We're going to dig deep into this in

Part 1. I want to hammer this point in one more way. After you've finished this chapter, I want you to close your eyes for a moment and I want you to think about this:

Imagine you're at an event, one of our trainings perhaps. There are 100 chiropractors and we're going out to lunch. We're standing on a very busy corner and we're all talking down the morning session. We're excited, and we're on a busy street. There are trucks and cars going 45 to 50 miles an hour and the street is five lanes wide. The signal is red, the little hand is up that means don't cross and we're just waiting for the little green guy to show up and give us the go-ahead, when out of the corner of your eye you see a little girl.

She appears to be around three years old. You notice that she's transfixed on a butterfly that's flying into the middle of the street. You're in the middle of a conversation when you see her take a step off of the sidewalk and into oncoming traffic. Her parent is looking the other direction, while this innocent little girl steps into what is going to be certain tragedy. What do you do? Just close your eyes. What do you do?

Now, I've asked this question live hundreds of times. I've asked it on webinars and trainings thousands of times, and the answer is always the same. Now maybe I just hang around good people like you, but the answer is *always,* I do whatever it takes. I save her life. I jump in the way. I grab her. I dive after her. I yell and move toward her.

You don't think about your family. You don't think about, *what will they say? What if I'm wrong? What if I fail? What if I miss? I didn't say I love you to my spouse before I left today, I've got three kids at home and they're more important. How much is this going to cost and how long is this going to take?*

The fact of the matter is, you don't ask any questions, you **do**.

You take immediate action. You grab the girl, you save her life and you are the hero, but you're just a human being. Why take the risk? Because we all share the belief that the sanctity of human life, especially that of an innocent young child, is of ultimate value in this world. That belief instilled within you is what drives you.

It will drive you to take action and save that little girl. This confirms your beliefs: *I'm a good human being. I love humanity. I love kids. I'm so happy that I was able to do that.* But there is a massive contradiction here: we're afraid to have a conversation with a mom about the healthcare of her kids. Whether it's an ear infection, sensory processing disorder, colic or whatever.

We're afraid to tell someone to bring in their spouse who suffers from allergies or asthma or migraines. We are afraid to tell someone who has beaten the crap out of their back for 40 years and is now complaining that can't drive off the tee, what it's actually going to take to get better. We are afraid to talk to them for fear that they might judge us. They might not like us, they might think we are after their money.

We're not afraid to jump into traffic and risk our own lives and never see our own families again because we are driven by a belief. Yet, we are afraid we will not take those actions in chiropractic. Why? Because we haven't identified and clarified our true belief system as it relates to chiropractic. When we do this, which we will in this book, everything will change.

Everything.

3 THE RESULT

"FUZZY TARGETS DON'T GET HIT."

-DR. DAVID JACKSON

This is a book about communication.

Not just any communication, but communication that will increase the perception of value in your community so you can build the practice of your dreams, serve the people around you and build an Epic life for yourself. It's a big task, but it is one hundred percent doable with the core strategy I'm about to share with you.

The strategy you must have is *clarity* in the result: find out *WHY* you're going to put in the work that it takes to become a better communicator. That is the target. That is the result.

What can you expect? Well, I want you to imagine all the different elements that go into the process of communication. Communication is not just what you say, it's what your practice conveys. It's your brand message. It's your marketing. It's the paint on your wall. If experts are right and they say that 85% of communication is nonverbal, then it's the space *between* the words that matters more than the words themselves.

The result MUST be clear. And oh, they're clear when you DO the work and identify your chiro BS: your chiropractic belief systems. They're clear when you begin to truly embrace and understand the Socratic process of getting people in your community to look at their BS: their belief systems.

When you get good at judging the gap between your belief, *what they need* and their belief, *what they currently want* and bring them together, only then will you have a clear definition of *exactly* what it's going to take to get this person face down so you can serve them, save them, and help them live up to their potential.

The result you're looking for will be different from the result I'll be looking for. But that's not the important thing here. The important thing for you to understand is that you must define the result you're after. **Fuzzy**

targets don't get hit. This has to be clear. What do you want?

Again, if you say, *I just want to grow my practice, I want to serve more people,* or *I want people to stick around longer,* those answers aren't going to cut it. How *many* people do you want to serve? You could always change your goals. How long do you want people to stick around? What do you want your OVA to be? How much money do you want in your bank account as a result of becoming a better Epic communicator inside your practice in your community? Clarity is where the game is won when it comes to result.

Let me paint a picture for you.

Imagine for a moment, that when you walk into practice on a Monday morning, the people scheduled (as many as you visualize) *want* to be there. They're not there just because they want to feel better, they're there because they believe in the same things you do. They *want* to be there because they know you are the authority. You are the credible expert. You've become a celebrity in your community.

They know they're in the right place.

They want to be there because they understand that yes, they feel better, but ultimately, they're expressing a higher potential for themselves and their family. So, they want to be there with all of their family members and their friends.

Your team wants to be there because they're no longer stuck in a "Billy Bob Back Pain" chiropractic office where everything revolves around pain-based wants. Your staff is inspired and trained and connected to the passion and the mission and the vision in ways you've only dreamed of.

Imagine for a minute that as people flood into your practice and lay face down, they have a clear expectation of the experience you're going to provide them. They know they're not there to just take up your time. They're there to get their nervous system checked, adjusted and tuned up so they can go out and make a difference in their own lives and in their own world. That each and every one of them is on a plan. Not just some haphazard *we'll see how you feel* plan, which allows the inmates to run the asylum. But an actual *plan,* because you know through your beliefs, your actions, and your results what they need, and you're delivering exactly that.

Imagine that these people (regardless of insurance benefits) are on a plan. They've either prepaid for their care, or they're on a monthly care plan for themselves and their family, and they gladly pay that fee every month, just like they do their DIRECTV bill, their cell phone bill, their car payment, and their insurance, because they understand the contribution it makes to their life.

Imagine that those same people stay with you for generations. You start seeing their kids and then their grandkids. Imagine that the stress you used to have from chasing and finding new people is gone because you finally realized that *if they knew you knew, they'd do what you do.* Through your new improved ability to be an Epic communicator, they now know what you know, and now do what you do.

You're probably saying to yourself, come on Dr. David is this really how it is? Not necessarily... but it can be. It's what happened to me in my practice, in my community and for thousands of other chiropractors who I've guided through this process to see this come to fruition.

Right now, we have a community of hundreds of docs we train with every week, and I watch it happen every day. To all of them? Nope. To most of them? Yes, because it still depends on the truth. It depends on the action.

You've got to begin with the result you were looking for first. Clarity. Conciseness. What do you *really* want at the end of the day? Not what your previous teachers and preachers and parents and gurus and coaches and colleagues told you could have. Be courageous. Have the freaking audacity to say, *this is what I WANT.*

You don't have to know how to get there yet. That's a process and a journey that's exciting. But you must have the confidence to say, *dammit this is what I WANT, and I am going to figure out how to use my skill set to communicate and my value to create that.*

Doc, here's another bottom line. Most people, including well-intentioned chiropractors, chase people and they chase money. I don't mean that in a negative sense, but they look in their bank account, they look at their bills, they look at their future, where they want to travel, the homes they want to build, and the college they want to send their kids to. Then they look at their student loan debt and they say, *how can I increase income?*

That's the wrong question to ask.

The right question to ask is, *how can I increase the value I contribute to the most amount of people possible, and then deliver on that value?*

When you ask that question, when you focus on increasing your value and when you focus on the perception of value, when you actually *train* on your communication instead of just working inside your practice, when you go through this book and you dog-ear it and you underline it and you challenge it and you challenge yourself, when you do that and you focus on costs, you don't need to worry about how many commas are in your bank account. They will be there. All you have to do is put a law of exchange in place.

It's time to visualize the result that was beaten out of you years ago. It's time to connect back to exactly what you want as you go through each of the three parts of this book.

Doc, that is your homework right now. Begin the process of redefining exactly what you want, and then change your focus from *I don't know how to do that* to, *I need to find out who I need to become and what I need to believe to achieve this process.*

What was *my* ultimate result? **Epic Practice.**

PART

OUR CHIRO BS

"WE GOT INTO CHIROPRACTIC TO CHANGE THE WORLD. INSTEAD, WE HAVE ALLOWED THE WORLD TO CHANGE US."

-REGGIE GOLD

We could go on and on about all of the BS that resides within this profession.

I'm sure you agree with me on this point. I've been there, done that. I've been a practicing chiropractor, and I've been a representative for state and national associations. I've started associations, I've run philosophy groups, I've spoken all over the world and I've coached thousands of chiropractors.

It gives me a certain perspective that you may or may not have. Regardless, I think we can agree that many chiropractors spend more hours on Facebook, griping and moaning about how bad the profession and all of its BS is than they do engaging with and actually serving the population. We're not going to waste our time in this book talking about that form of BS. Although, one thing that has always struck me as the biggest contradiction, is how this profession that is supposed to be based upon connection is so damn disconnected.

Many years ago when I started Epic Practice, one of the most important things for me was to create a community. To create an environment that was not just full of strategies, resources and growth, but to create one that was full of crowdsourcing. It wasn't about me, it was about everyone inside, connected and helping one another. It's what I'm proudest of in my 30 years of being a chiropractor.

In the following chapters, we're going to dig into a different type of BS. We're going to dig into the chiropractic Belief Systems.

Now, it's obvious that I cannot understand exactly what your belief systems are, at least not in the context of the written word. Some of the things I describe to you may apply, some of them may not, but they each earn their spot on these pages because they are the most prominent and preeminent challenges to the belief systems of the profession at large.

As you go through this process, do yourself a favor, don't be a know it all. Don't act as if you've already gone through this process before. Even if you already have, look at it with a fresh set of eyes, a fresh mind and a fresh heart.

Why is this so important?

We have so many preconceived ideas and beliefs that we're not aware of or that might not be true. Concepts that someone respectable taught us in school, or that came from a previous chiropractor, something learned in a seminar, or came from something we were coached on in the past. It's not about judging whether they're right or wrong or whether or not you are, this is about looking at an actual belief system and asking a very simple question. It's the same question I asked my daughters while they were growing up and still do to this day.

As they were growing up, I watched them struggle. Yet, instead of trying to fix the struggles for them, instead of trying to take their struggles away, I wanted to give them the life skills and necessary tools to deal with their own struggles and take responsibility for them. I asked them this simple question:

How's it working for you?

I'm going to ask you to think about this question when we go through each one of these six belief systems that are prevalent in chiropractic: how is it working for you?

If the answer is, *it's great,* then move on. If the answer is, *could be better,* then dig in. Our belief systems dictate our behaviors and our behaviors dictate our results. My personal belief is that W.A.S. or "What's at Stake" is life itself.

I'm long past the notion that this is simply about helping people feel better. Though that's important, it's about helping people function better. It's about helping people heal better. When you master this process and have strong belief systems, you're able to communicate better to others, which in turn allows them to make better decisions. I believe this is worth all of the effort, all of the time, all of the energy and all of the investment you can muster up.

So, if you're ready to rock n' roll, let's clear up some BS.

4 WHAT THEY WANT

"CAN I SUPERSIZE THAT?"

-MODERN MAN

When I ask you what a patient wants from you, how would you respond?

I've posed this question to thousands of chiropractors and I've never heard a more shining example of what I like to call "chiro exaggeration" mixed in with a little bit of manipulation. Answers such as, *well they want to be healthier, they want to live up to their God-given potential, or they want to live with a nervous system free of interference.*

Blah, blah, blah. That's what *we* want. I'll ask you again, what do *they* want?

It's actually three very simple things.

Whether it's Mary with her migraine, Susan with her child that has an ear infection, Bob with a sinus infection, Jimmy with the flu, or Billy with a backache, everyone who walks into your practice wants the same thing: to feel better, yesterday, and to have someone else pay for it. That's what they want.

The challenge is that we chiropractors try to give them what they want. It's a challenge because it's impossible. What chiropractors want underneath it all, is to be liked. That's not a chiropractic thing- that's called being human. We all want to be liked.

When their want to feel better, yesterday, and have someone else pay for it meets our want of wanting to be liked, we create an agreement that says, *I'm going to do everything I can to have you feeling better as quickly as possible AND we'll bill the insurance for you.*

The problem is, while that sounds simple, it simply doesn't work.

When I sat down with Mary back in 1989 and I couldn't look her in the eye (the story you know and the reason I quit chiropractic) it was because I couldn't tell her the truth.

It wasn't that I had a hard time telling the truth. I knew what she wanted and I knew I couldn't give it to her. I could've told her *maybe*. I had patients whose headaches went away and I had patients whose headaches didn't go away. But I was giving Mary my word. I was looking into her eyes and I was saying, *we got this. I can help you feel better as quickly as possible. We'll go ahead and take care of that payment and the insurance billing for you.*

I couldn't do it anymore. I couldn't look her in the eye, Doc. We can't give people what they want but man, we try. We try and we try, and our attempts are furthered by the good intentions (for the most part) of coaches, gurus, seminars, trainers and leaders out there who say *well, here's how you get it done.*

Enter scare tactics.

Well Mary, you know that if you don't get this taken care of now, you're going to be ten times worse ten years from now. Harry, you're going end up in a wheelchair at this pace. Where do you think you're going to be?

If you hold a gun to someone's head and threaten their future, they'll part with their money and do what you say. You can talk anyone into a year-long care plan if you use coercion, scare tactics, and manipulation... but that's not BEing Epic. That's not what you want to do.

Instead, we need to reposition them so they recognize it's not about what they want, it's about what they *need*.

What they *want* is to feel better yesterday and have someone else pay for it. What they *need* is to function better as often as possible and take responsibility for that for the rest of their life.

WHAT THEY WANT ———————— WHAT THEY NEED

Take a look above. You see the gap between what they want and what they need? That gap is where your practice dies. More importantly, it's where *they* die.

It's where they go back to the medical system. Back to the drugs, back to the bad food, back to the bad habits, back to the things that got them there in the first place. People *want* to supersize their Biggie Mac and get a 64-ounce cola along with it. But that's not what they *need*.

The reason they're in your practice is because so many people just gave them what they want.

Massages, antibiotics (drugs that don't address the cause of the problem) and care plans that say, *oh sure I can treat you two or three times and you'll feel better. Come back when it hurts again.* They've been given what they want so many times and for so long, that by the time they get to you they're an absolute train wreck of a situation.

Do you know what they really, truly *want* underneath it all? They want someone to tell them the truth.

But it can't be my truth. It has to be your truth. You'll have look at what they want and be able to honestly say, I believe what they need is to function better and I'm going to have to learn how to develop beliefs about what that actually means. We'll talk about that in an upcoming chapter, but it's crucial that you remember they need to function better as often as possible.

All of this has to do with the "essence of time" and what that means. We'll cover that later along with how to take responsibility for and honestly look at the gap. When you really look at it, you can see that it's not only a place where nine practices died, but it's also a place where practices and people grow and live.

What communication and the truth will do (when done in an Epic way) is grow your practice by getting people to actually *want* what they *need*.

It's a skill set that I developed for myself and that I want to share with you. It's important for you to understand, at this early stage, that this skill set will create millions of dollars in additional revenue over the course of your career. More importantly, this skill set will be the cause of millions of dollars which in turn will affect the lives of hundreds, thousands, even tens of thousands of people in your community.

When you can masterfully close the gap, not through manipulation tactics but by influence and get people to look at their own BS their own belief systems, that's when you get people to say, *what I want is to function better, as often as possible, and I'm willing to take responsibility and pay cash for that.*

If that sounds too good to be true, then you're in the right place.

I'm going to prove it to you and show you the process of communicating value so that patients pay, stay and refer.

5 OPQRST

"THE MOST IMPORTANT THING IN COMMUNICATION IS HEARING WHAT ISN'T SAID."

-PETER DRUCKER

Years ago, I was listening to a music professor and they said something I'll never forget.

They said: *The music you enjoy is not enjoyable because of the words or the notes, but more so because of the space between the words, and the space between the notes.*

In my early years in practice, Mary would come in with a headache. I'd read her consultation form to find out who referred her and then looked at the purpose of her visit which said: I've had these migraines for six years and they start on the right side, they go into the back of my head and up into my eye. I've taken Advil®, ibuprofen, Imitrex®, I've had shots, I've been to the hospital, I've tried two chiropractors, I've been to physical therapists and the list went on and on and on.

As a well-intentioned chiropractor I thought okay, Mary is here because she has headaches and of course what she wants is to feel better yesterday and have someone else pay for it. Yet, the belief system I had then is the one that most chiropractors have now, and it's one that leads them to believe that Mary is there because of her headaches.

This is a critical flaw. Mary is not there because of her headaches. Mary is there because her headaches have caused her to lose something or are preventing her from pursuing something of much higher value. I want to restate that: Mary isn't there because she has a headache, the headache is causing something. It's the effect she is concerned about.

Mary is there because her headaches have taken something away from her that is of high enough value that she called my office and fueled up her car. She got a babysitter, put dinner on the table and then she drove to my office and waited there for an hour. She has enough value in the things she lost, that she wants them back. That or she's placing value in the thing she wants to attain but has been unable to because of the headaches. The critical flaw is that we buy their BS that they're there for a headache.

Think about it, Doc. Mary had headaches for six years. She shows up and you say, *all right, how long have you had them?* And she responds, *for six years.*

P. Does anything *provoke* them?
Q. What's the *quality* sharp, dull?

Look, we're doing what we were taught because that's what we believe is necessary.

Step back for a moment. Not that that's wrong, but back up just for a moment and look at Mary. She's had headaches for six years. The question that immediately pops into my mind is, why today? *Well, because I'm just tired.* I don't buy it. Why? There's a process called "the seven layers of why." It's out of the context of this book, but it involves asking people why until you get to the truth.

Why today? *Well, because I had a bad one last week.* Well, why, what happened? *Well, you know I have this x and this y.* Just keep asking again, again and again. Usually by the time you get to level three or four (certainly if you happen to get to seven) you can actually find out the truth.

Mary has had these headaches for six years, but she came to me today. Why? Because I saw her at a talk. Why? Because I met her at a spinal screening and so on, but maybe there's something deeper going on here.

Early on in practice, I just bought it for what it was. She has headaches. I know what she wants and I'll do what I can. We already know how that story went for me and I'm sure you have your own version of how it's going for you right now.

We can see how it's going for the profession, but what if we shifted our beliefs?

What if we wanted a different result and looked for a different action? What if I did my consultation and report of findings differently, so I would get a different conversion? The result was I didn't just convert people to see how it would go after a couple of adjustments: I created a care plan that was consistent with my beliefs.

Imagine for a moment that you have a different belief system that drives those actions and behaviors and gets you that result.

There's something more to the story. Using the Socratic method, I might ask, *Mary, you have been dealing with this for a long time. Why did you come to me today?* She will respond with a story, and what I do with that story will absolutely determine the outcome and growth in my practice. When we get into Chapter 16, I'm going to teach you exactly how to take it from the point where you think *I'm not buying it, that's not why she's here today* to then be able to communicate your version of the truth to Mary. That way, when you get her face down on your table, what she wants is now what she needs.

See, we were taught that we're supposed to go through a process of OPQRST. Then we're supposed to poke the pain and say, *does it hurt right here?* Then we're supposed to X-ray the area of pain and say *okay, everything looks good* or *you've got a reverse curve,* etc. Again, none of this is bad, it just is. Maybe you were taught to do some orthopedic test and then document that process. Maybe you were taught to take their symptoms and then follow the scripts and the protocols to say, *yes Mary, I can help you get rid of your pain.*

But that belief system has you acting that way and has you building a pain and insurance-based practice. If that's what you want, then you've already got the answers. You can close the book and move on.

If what you're looking for is a wellness-based lifestyle practice, if what you're looking for is people who truly understand, not hypothetically, but truly understand the idea, the process and the value of functioning at a higher level through a clear nervous system from this day on and for the rest of their lives. If people truly understand that, then you've created a complete and different world. It all starts with the BS idea that we're supposed to hunt down the symptom and then we're supposed to follow up on it. Here's how that looks on visit six:

How are you doing today Mary?

Well you know, I'm not doing that well. I still have my headaches... this is not working.

They're thinking it, you're thinking it and you're thinking you can't go on like this. You're thinking *maybe I should refer you out or maybe I should put more ice on it, for 25 minutes instead of 20, or maybe I should use this therapy instead of that, or maybe I should sell you these vitamins instead of those and so on.* Again, I'm not judging the process we've all been through. Do what you know how to do but address the cause. I'm not even talking about the subluxation (yeah, I'm going to use the S word) or the spinal lesion or whatever it is you were taught. I'm not talking about that cause, I'm talking about the belief system cause.

You're following a system: where's the pain? There it is. I found it. I see it. Does it still hurt? *Oh, it hurts there now.* Okay, well let me adjust you, how do you feel? *Well it feels a little better, but I think it's coming from right over here.* Actually, go lay back down and so on and so forth and all of the sudden, you're dialing for dollars. You're hitting the high spots, racking and cracking them and hoping (as a strategy) that enough people will feel better, so you can maintain your reputation and your practice.

Doc, that sucks.

That's not what we're here for. Go through the BElief Triangle.

What have your beliefs been? About Day 1, or Day 2? About OPQRST? It's highly likely that you are making this mistake with a new patient: They call in, you schedule to see them and on Day 1 you talk to them, you X-ray them, you examine them and you tell them what's going on. You tell them you've found the problem and you adjust them because you just want to alleviate their pain. While I understand the empathy behind that act, you have to understand the mistake in that very act.

If what you're trying to do is get someone to understand the value of long-term care. If they've had a headache for six years, then they can wait until tomorrow when your new beliefs will bring about new actions. You're going to go through a process. You'll get them to go from caring about what they *wanted*, to feel better yesterday and have someone else pay for it, to helping them understand what they *need*.

That is *precisely* what we're going to do all throughout Part 3, but you've got to identify this belief FIRST. Make a new triangle.

If the result is, *I want people to better understand the value of long-term care and live up to their potential,* then what actions what behaviors am I going to enact? What am I going have to change as it relates to the consultation? This is an area where people really get stuck. We think, *it's my job to make them feel better, so I've got to talk about it on every visit and then back it up. Then somehow down the line, I have to convince them that <u>now</u> it's time to talk about being well and teach them how to maintain that wellness so they don't get worse.*

The same old crap, Doc. It's proven it doesn't work.

What *does* work is converting *wants* to *needs,* which is precisely what's going to happen when you identify your beliefs and create new, more powerful beliefs to supersede the ones that are limiting you.

6 TIME ≠ MONEY

> "THE PERSON BORN WITH A TALENT THEY ARE MEANT TO USE WILL FIND THEIR GREATEST HAPPINESS IN USING IT."
>
> *-JOHANN WOLFGANG VON GOETHE*

One of the belief systems I struggled with greatly was the idea of time. From a young age, I was taught that time equals money. This concept was reaffirmed throughout chiropractic school and again in the chiropractic world. I was taught that time amounted to quality, and therefore more time equaled more quality.

As a person rooted in integrity who wanted to be liked, trusted and respected by my patients, I took that literally and spent around 45 minutes with each patient. Looking back, I honestly don't know what I did with or for them, but I thought it was necessary based on my belief system at the time because quality is based upon how much time I spend... right?

This is a sticking point for anyone who is looking at capacity. You've seen it. You've felt it. You hear about a doctor that sees a large volume of patients and the first thing people say is *well, they can't possibly be giving them quality care.* This doesn't happen just in chiropractic, either. Take a look at different industries and you'll find the same kind of people that share the same belief system. Why? Because we live in a world where people *do* trade their time for money: *I'll give you 60 minutes, you give me my $20.*

In chiropractic, however, that belief is not true.

Now, if you still buy into that belief system (even though it's not true) it'll cause you to behave in a certain way and produce results that you're most likely not going to be very happy with.

What's actually true? In chiropractic, we trade *talent* for money.

There's a dramatic difference between the two. Once I had a major "come to Jesus" moment and finally ditched the, *you need to spend this much time for this and spend this much time for that* BS my mother-father-teachers-preachers told me, the difference was suddenly crystal clear.

I'm going to have you do the same thing right now.

Let's imagine for a moment that I meet you at an event somewhere. Maybe it's at our annual Epic Impact Event and I say, *Doc, can you check me real quick before I go on the stage?* And you say, *sure, there's a table right here.* How long will it take? How long does it take when your husband or wife or one of your kids says, *will you check me before I walk to school?* And you say, *of course.* How long is that going to take?

The answer is a couple of minutes- tops.

The question is, are you going to give me worse service than you would your patients because I'm not paying you and we're at an event? Are you going to serve your kids and give them less of an adjustment? Are you going to give your spouse an inferior adjustment? Or are you going to share all your talents as quickly as possible and let them be on their way to live their lives?

You know the answer, but here's the contradiction: the reason we do it is because when it's for our own family or colleagues we say, *it's my talent- I'll share with you,* and there's not an exchange of money. When money enters into the conversation we say, *it's $50. Wow. I can't possibly deliver the talent in two minutes and accept $50. I don't feel right about that.* So what I'm going to do is I'm going to put on some hot packs and then I'm going to stretch out a little bit. Maybe I'll give them a little massage, maybe I'll paint their fingernails or wax their car for them. I'm obviously being sarcastic here, but the point is that we figure out things to do under the guise of necessity.

Again, I'm not placing judgment if that's your game. But for most of us, we're covering up because we don't believe in the value of our talent. Because again, we're so used to exchanging *time* for money.

Consider the following scenario for a moment: Your young son or daughter broke their arm and has to have unavoidable emergency surgery.

One surgeon says they are going to reduce the fracture, meaning they have to go in and plate their arm, like I had done when I was 15 years old. The surgeon says, *we can't put your child under general anesthesia because they just ate, so we are going to have to do a block* (which is also what happened to me). Your child going to be awake during this process and it's going to take two and a half hours, at a cost of $5,000 per hour.

If another, equally skilled orthopedic surgeon comes in and says, *you know we can't put your son/daughter under general anesthesia so we're going to have to do a local block, but I'll get in and out of there and make this thing better than new in 15 minutes for $12,000.*

Which one are you going to take? Which one do you want? You want less time, less pain, less suffering. You're going to pay the extra money.

See, the difference between time and talent has been blurred because we were taught that we trade our time. Our patients come to us and we know what they want. Well, they want to feel better, yesterday, and have someone else pay for it, and they want a minute of your time, right? But *you* have a belief system that you are actually capable of engaging in, questioning and changing if you need to.

That's the process I went through. I've seen hundreds, I've seen thousands of chiropractors go through that process and break free. Because here's a different belief system, I believe that time is the *only* thing we cannot change and never get back.

I believe (these are just my beliefs, so try them on for size see if they fit) that time is *so valuable*, that the faster I can get you in my practice to do exactly what I need to do in order to get you out back into the life that brought you here in the first place, the more valuable my services are to you. I believe "Mildred" most likely belongs in another chiropractor's office, because if "Mildred" wants to sit down with me for 45 minutes it's probably not the right place for her.

That's okay, because I'm not trying save everyone. I can't, but I'm going to save the people that are swimming toward me, like the US Coast Guard does. I believe that if it takes me 63 seconds to assess and correct the interferences I find in that person, and I take 64 seconds, I just robbed them of a second of their life they'll never get back. I believe that those seconds add up to minutes, those minutes adds up to hours, those hours add up to weeks, those weeks add up to months and those months turn into years and so on. Over the course of my career I'm going to save myself, and more importantly my community and my patients, months and months of time.

See, I don't share in the belief system that time is money. I believe that *talent* is money.

I believe the more of an authority I am, the more credible I am, the better results I get and the more of a celebrity I become in my own community as a chiropractor. More value is exchanged when they work with me. As a result, I see that wow, I can serve a lot more than 20 patients, can't I? How do I go from a high of seeing nine patients a day (because I thought I was doing the right thing) to seeing nine patients in a 20-minute time slot?

It's easy, I reshuffled.

I really looked at my belief systems and I said well, here's what I believe but it's not working for me. Is there another truth I can accept so I can get rid of the limiting one and add in the positive, growth-based truth?

The truth for me is really clear. Talent is what I want.

I want to go to a restaurant that doesn't have any empty tables. I want to wait in line to go get that reservation because that's where the best thing is happening. People want to see you succeed and they want to see you busy. They will invest the time and the money into that as long as *you* invest that time and the money into yourself. You have to reevaluate your beliefs and replace them with positive, uplifting, growth-oriented beliefs to create the value they'll be willing to exchange because they now *want* what they *need*.

7 I'LL HAVE TO ASK MY SPOUSE...

> "MONEY WILL NOT PURCHASE HAPPINESS FOR THE MAN WHO HAS NO CONCEPT OF WHAT HE WANTS."
>
> *-AYN RAND*

There are very few areas of practice that create as much friction and stress as fees and finance. From setting your fees, to care plans, to payment options, to insurance reimbursement: all of this creates such a cloud in the otherwise simple process of running a business. It does so because once again, we have a limited belief system that has been passed down by those before us.

That belief system comes across in many different ways: *I have to accept insurance because everyone has it, I can't afford care, I live on a budget, my CA couldn't afford care, the economy is down, you don't understand that people in my community*...blah, blah, blah.

The truth behind most of this is that as a profession we have valued pain relief based upon the fact that a third party will typically reimburse it to some degree. As that third-party insurance gets harder and harder to get, pays less and less and fewer and fewer people have it, we are forced to become honest and truthful about what values we are actually exchanging.

The bottom line is, we have to put our philosophical differences aside.

If Mary comes back into the office with her migraine and I say, *it's going to take $1,200 to initially help you with that migraine,* that's a hell of a lot of Advil®. That's a lot of massages. That's a lot of money for one small thing: to get rid of her headache.

The biggest problem we face in chiropractic right now with our conversion results (which end up in a retention of between nine and twelve lifetime visits for someone) is that our behavior when doing our care plans basically says, *I think I can help, we'll adjust you a few times and we'll see how it goes.*

We're doing that because we don't have the belief system (like we talked about earlier and will continue to talk about) and in addition, we haven't learned the exchange of value system that needs to be put into place.

We are coming across as if we're selling them an extremely overpriced, stickier Band-Aid or a big ass bottle of chiro aspirin. The way they're looking at it is, I could spend $50 here to get rid of my headache or you're asking me to spend $1,500 here to get rid of my headache. Looking back on Chapters 4 and 5 you'll see that all of this starts digging us into a deeper hole.

My gosh, I hope you're starting to feel better right now.

The process of trying to run a chiropractic business this way is extremely difficult. To try to convince someone that what they *want* is worth X number of dollars and they don't need insurance if they don't have it. The best in the *world* have a hard time doing that, let alone the average chiropractor.

But what if we shifted our focus? What if we shifted the value transaction?

What if you actually started with the belief that people will pay for the things they value. That people will invest in their bigger future. That a mother and a father will do anything, drive any distance, spend any amount of time and invest any amount of money (even if they have to borrow it) into their child if it's based upon a clear and concise predicted outcome.

Once again the challenge is, is this the headache or the ear infection, the sinus problem or the backache? Is that the value that they're willing to exchange? In my humble opinion and given my experiences, hell no. That's not it.

There's so much more.

And once again, we're going to nail that down deeply in Part 3. But here in our chiropractic belief systems we need to look at the *idea* of what money is, as well as the role it plays in chiropractic. The bottom line is this: money itself is pictures of dead presidents printed on pieces of paper.

By itself, money means nothing.

Money is just a more convenient way of saying *hey, I need a pig and you need a clay pot. I've got a clay pot, you have a pig so let's barter and exchange*. Money simplified the exchange. What money is, is the best in *you* exchanged for the best in *me* and vice versa. What money is, is stored value. What money represents is the talent we were talking about in the last chapter. What money does not represent, in this case, is the time or the promise. It is the talent. It is the idea, it is that I know when *not* to adjust, I know where *not* to do things. I know exactly *how* to do things.

We don't need to go into all of that "doctory" stuff, but your belief system is something you've got to own first, because you can't sell something you don't own. You can't even rent it out if you don't own it. The belief system we have to adopt is that the care you're going to sell (and I'm using that word intentionally because I know it ruffles feathers) is so valuable that they will find a way to get the job done.

That value may not be there when someone agrees that their care plan is based upon a headache or something else, but it will be there when we teach you how to close the gap and communicate the truth. In Part 3 I can promise you this: the value will be there as long as you believe it. Then, when you have the communication tools to help them see the value in their bigger future, in their potential and not just the improvement of their pain and symptoms, the whole world changes because now they will *gladly* pay.

How do I know this? Because I went from stuck, struggling, broke and quitting after realizing I didn't want to deal with insurance, to accepting 100% cash in the 90s long before it was popular. It certainly wasn't necessary because insurance was really good at the time, but I was compelled to develop my communication skills to such a level of expertise that even people with insurance would say, *I get it. That's awesome, thank you.*

That was my goal. To get them to thank me for charging them cash. I didn't give care away. I didn't do unlimited care at a fixed fee. I didn't play games with people. I charged good money and people embraced it.

I delivered value.

It was still *under* price because I *over* delivered. Doc, that process of moving forward hasn't just stayed with me. I cannot tell you how many young chiropractors and old chiropractors alike come out and say, *well I'd love to be less pain oriented and more wellness oriented and I'd love to do less insurance, but I just I don't really see anybody doing that.* Oh my gosh.

Last year in our Epic community I saw around one dozen practices hit seven figures for the first time. That's one million dollars, two commas, 100% cash. People who are delivering chiropractic care who aren't selling anything on the side (and that's cool if you want to do that) but I'm talking about delivering care to people for a good valuable fee. They're not just giving it away. They're not crazy busy, they're not making eighty-thousand a week or anything, but they've got a great business model.

They're working smart... for cash.

They have more freedom than ever, but they're working hard when they're in the office. They're working on their practice, they're working on the stuff I'm talking about in this book and they've gone cash.

They've stayed away from insurance. It simplifies your life and it removes so many hurdles. It empowers you. You don't have to play the frickin' games. You know you don't have to pay people to process. You don't have to risk reimbursement audits. There's a freedom that comes from the mindset of *I want to go cash.*

The reason you want to go cash but you haven't yet, is because you don't believe that people will pay for it. You've got to look at that belief and ask, *where does it come from?* Then you've got to simply change it. The way I'm suggesting you begin this process right now, today, is not to say you want to go cash tomorrow. It has to be today. You have to believe *today* that people will pay any amount of money for what they value most.

Here's the question: If (especially if you have children, if you don't just imagine you are a parent) if your child really needed something, I mean *really* needed it to be healthy, happy, and safe, what lengths would you go to?

Every parent will say they'll do anything. Even if they know it's not going to be easy, the answer is still *anything.*

My youngest daughter (who is 21) struggled when she was in high school. She didn't struggle with the school work. She struggled with *school*. She didn't fit in. She's the youngest of three sisters, all of whom we raised to be very independent, brilliant badasses. And that's exactly what she was (and is even more so now) so she couldn't stand all the games. I mean, I grew up with all boys so I didn't realize the level of cruelty girls are capable of.

She knew it was all BS and didn't want anything to do with it. The experiences she had early on in high school began to impact her negatively. Witnessing how teens interacted with one another disturbed her to her core. It wasn't like, *oh I'm entitled get me out of here.* In her own words it was more like, *I'm so disappointed with my generation.*

It began to get heavier and heavier until it eventually got to a point where she asked if she could drop out of school. We all knew that wasn't going to be an option, but what were the options then? We tried several, and what we landed on was a unique school that had one teacher for one student. One on one.

She was happier and healthier. She was progressing and learning better than ever before. She crushed her high school years and she did it in style. She received a better education than either we or the high school could have given her, but it wasn't inexpensive. One teacher, one child. It was a huge investment I happily paid for every single month. It was a college tuition for high school and then some, but my wife and I didn't care.

We did it because we love our child.

Parents will do that for their children. They'll do it for themselves as long as the value is positioned away from feeling better, to *being* better. In this book, we're going to continue this process. We will help you by asking you to define *better*. Once you do, they will come.

They will pay and they will stay.

8 ONCE I HAVE... THEN I'LL...

> "A PRINCIPLE DOESN'T CARE WHETHER YOU BELIEVE IN IT OR NOT."
>
> -DR. DAVID JACKSON

I'm sure you're no stranger to some of the principles I've been sharing with you in this book. One of the principles, commonly referred to as the "Be, Do, Have" principle, is where the essence of the BElief triangle process came from. As with all principles, "Be, Do, Have" isn't just an idea. It's not just an opinion. It's a law.

In order to *have* something, you have to *do* something. In order to *do* something, you've got to *be* something. In order to get a result, you need to take action. In order to take action, you've got to believe. See where I'm going with this?

The interesting thing about a principle is that it doesn't care if you believe in it or not. The other interesting thing about a principle is that you can't fight it. You can try all day to jump up onto the roof of a thirty-story building, but gravity is a principle. It's a law and it's going to win every single time.

The same goes for this principle of BElief, BEhavior and the results of BE. But so many of us reverse the principle out of convenience. It often sounds like this:

Well, as soon as I have enough patients, then I'll do this activity, then I'll ask for referrals and then I'll be busy. Once I have the money, then I will take action and invest in a training program and then I'll be successful. Once I have the testimonial, then I'll talk to other people about it and then I'll be more popular. Once I have their respect, then I'll convert them into something else and I'll be content with their care plan. Once they understand how their pain is taken away through initial intensive care, then I'll take action and talk to them about wellness care and I'll be successful because people will move over to wellness care.

None of these things will ever work regardless of how hard you try because you are literally disobeying a law: the principles of cause and effect.

I want you to take a moment and think about any examples of when you have tried to reverse the law. Think about what would happen if you actually went about it in the proper order the principle required, instead of trying to bait and switch somebody. This is what so many chiropractors unknowingly do. They bring patients in on a special offer and then they say, *oh by the way, you need X-rays. The offer was $10, but you need $200 worth of X-rays.*

How does that leave someone feeling?

What are you communicating to that person when you do something like that? When it's a free offer or a discounted offer, but you gouge them on the X-rays? Or, you give them what they came in for and adjust them. You then recommend they come in three times a week, they say they are busy and you say okay, can you come in two times a week? You start negotiating with them and end up seeing them only once a week. You lose your power. You lost. You gave away your credibility and your certainty.

They win. You recommend a few visits, say you're going to relieve their pain and then you try to convert them to a wellness plan. Where do you think the often quoted saying of "I heard that once you go to a chiropractor, you always have to go" comes from? You think to yourself, *oh that's why I don't want to talk to people about long term care plans, because everyone knows that.*

Why do they know that?

They know that because you *didn't* talk to them about the value of long term care plans. You *didn't* get them to *want* what they need. You *didn't* communicate the value so well that they asked you for long term care. Are you that much smarter and that much richer than all of the people in your community? Are you the only one who deserves to be adjusted for rest of your life?

The answer is obviously no. But we've got to understand that we have to move forward with what we believe in and who we are before we take action and get results.

One of the best ways I can wrap up this concept is by reminding you of the idea we talked about in the last chapter, and even earlier in Chapters 4 and 5. It's an idea that permeates this entire book. It's the idea that many people take what I refer to as "The Easy-Hard Route."

People are going to come in with their headaches, but many chiropractors won't dig in to find out what's *really* limiting them. They won't try to find out what their patient has *really* lost and why. They won't say, *why today? Why did you decide today was the day to handle this problem you've had for six years?* The idea is that maybe it's not the headache itself.

Remember Mary from Chapter 5? Let's wrap that story up. Here's what happened:

Mary has her first child. She's a single, working mom so she has a nanny who comes in during the day while she's at work. Mary doesn't like it, but it's what she has to do. Mary's been trying to have a child for a long time. When she finally got pregnant, her relationship broke off and she was under an immense amount of stress.

So here she is, a single mother who doesn't know what to do or where to turn. She already feels like somewhat of a failure. She has to work to keep the family afloat, but she doesn't want to. She has to leave her baby alone at home and to top it all off she has intense migraine headaches. She comes home from a long day at work and the baby starts pulling on her ear. The nanny says that the baby has been pulling on her ear a lot and she's been crying, fussing, won't eat and won't take the bottle.

Mary suspects she has an ear infection and thinks to herself *what am I going to do?* Mary's feeling guilty, but her migraine is so severe that she says *okay, I'm just going to change her and try to get her a bottle, but then I've got to lay down for a few minutes.* She literally collapses.

She wakes up three hours later in an absolute state of panic and fear. As she awakens, she bolts out of the room to find her precious little girl covered in snot, her diaper is dirty, and she's screaming her heart out. In that moment, as Mary reaches over to apologize to her little girl for abandoning her, Mary thinks: *I'm a horrible mom.*

Mary calls your office and makes an appointment for the next day. She tells the front desk that she has a headache and you believe her. When she visits you, your whole conversation is about Mary's headache even though the real reason Mary came to your practice is because she feels like she's not a good mom.

Knowing the truth of why Mary came in today, I'm going to focus the conversation around enabling her to be the *best* mom.

The conversation will be about how I want to increase that potential for her and her child so she can feel confident and secure so she can heal better, feel better and be a better mom. Which conversation is going to give you more value? Mary *will* go on my care plan. I can promise you that. I closed 90 - 95% of my care plans every single time (cash) regardless of how much money they had or did not have.

Why? Because I offered value.

But see, that's hard. That's not easy. It's easy to accept the headache. It's easy to say, *oh you have insurance?*

Great, we absolutely accept it and the copay is $12. That's easy. It's easy when they say, *I'm a single mom and I'm really busy* to back down and go from seeing them three times a week to only seeing them once. It's easy when people say, *wait a minute, that adjustment helped, but what about this pain down here?* It's easy to say, *well lay back down. Let me check it again.* It's easy when people want an immediate fix for their pain and you simply give them that.

It's easy to do all of that. Just like it's easy to walk around the elephant in the room.

It's easy, but damn, it gets harder later on doesn't it? It gets really hard later when you have to address it. It gets really hard when Mary stops showing up and you ask you front desk, *where'd Mary go?* That's hard. It gets really hard when Mary does feel better, and you know you need to keep it going because you don't want her progress to unwind and go back to how bad it was before.

You try to scare Mary. It gets hard. It gets really hard when the insurance runs out and she goes from paying twelve dollars a visit to sixty. It gets really hard, but most chiropractors choose the "Easy-Hard" route and it kills them. And it kills this profession.

So, what if you flipped your belief?

What if you went through the hard things first? What if you chose to address the hard issues first so your life, your practice and your relationships were easier later? What if you sat down and drilled into Mary's mindset and moved her away from the *wants* towards the *needs*? What if you found out she felt like a bad mom and then built the value around that? What if you said:

I know you have insurance and it would be great if insurance covered the care you require, but it doesn't. It covers sickness and we're here working on your potential. We've kept our costs low by eliminating the BS middleman, because the insurance company doesn't actually care about your health. They just want your premiums and they want to make more than they spend. I don't want to be told what to do or how often to see you. I know what it's going to take. I work for you, not your insurance company and that's how we keep our fees affordable.

Instead of just pointing out her problems, what if I showed her the neurology behind what's happening to her while going over her care plan? I demonstrated what was wrong with her, and I told her we would re-examine her every twelve visits. We were never going to simply guess. She was going to know when and what I knew.

Here's what I would say to her:

There will be days when you feel wonderful and think wow, why am I here? There will be days when you feel like crap and go "this isn't working." Every single one of those days we will have a conversation about how we're going to move toward functioning better, not just feeling better. I care about you. I care about how you feel, but whether you feel good or bad isn't necessarily going to determine if I adjust you or to what degree. Just like if you get food poisoning and feel sick, it's actually your body's healthy response. It sucks that you have food poisoning, but it's really good that your body's getting rid of all that stuff. I know it feels like crap, but your body is actually saving its own life.

So, what if I actually *educated* my patients? What if I communicated with them from the very beginning? What if I told them about the value of wellness care from Day 1 and didn't bait and switch later?

What if I went at it hard-easy?

What if I address the issues in my relationships right when they happen, instead of waiting for them to fester and get worse? That's a belief situation isn't it? Well, let me tell you something, I shifted. I made a radical turn, and in turn I've helped hundreds and thousands of people do the same thing. It is an absolute game changer.

When you go hard-easy, you end up honoring the principle: this is who I am, and this is who I'm BEing, this is what I BElieve. I'm going to tell people the truth and I'm going to work so hard on my actions and my ability to actually communicate value and results. Do you want to know what the results are? Here's what they sound like:

You are so lucky. You are so, so lucky.

People are going to constantly say to you, you are so lucky in your practice. You're so lucky, you have such a beautiful relationship with your wife. You are so lucky. Your kids are so healthy, they are so intelligent, so kind and so respectful. Chiropractors often say to me, *you're so lucky you live in that big house, you travel the world, you take three months off a year when you practice. You're so lucky.*

Now, I just look at them and laugh on the inside because you know what? I believe patients are healthy by choice not by chance. I believe I am successful by choice, not by chance. I choose to believe in the things that are causal and I know how important it is to move forward with that belief in mind.

Look, there's a lot of chiropractic BS but none of it matters. The only thing that matters is your own chiropractic belief systems, **your chiropractic BS.**

We've just gone over a few of them. There's more, but these are the important ones. These are the ones that deserve your time and attention. These are the ones that you're going to struggle with and need to break through by using the BElief Triangle to create your own belief system.

You might find yourself asking, *what if a belief is unknown to me? How will I know if I'm unconscious of it?* To figure it out you'll have to look at the result. If the result isn't what you want, look at the actions to find out what's holding you back. What if you say, *I want more money* but deep down you believe money is the root of all evil because a parent told you that the rich and corporations rip people off? Is it a law that people who have money are bad people?

Or do we share the same belief that money simply expands who you are? If you're an asshole and get a lot of money, you're going to be a bigger asshole. If you're a philanthropist and a giver and make a lot of money, you're going to be a bigger philanthropist and a bigger giver.

What beliefs do you want to adopt? You've got to be firm with these, because in Part 2 it's time to shift into what *they* believe. We're going to talk about what *their* BS is. When you understand yours and theirs, then and only then, can we tell the truth.

PART
2

THEIR BS

"THE ART OF MEDICINE INVOLVES AMUSING THE PATIENT WHILE NATURE CURES THE DISEASE."

-VOLTAIRE

It should be abundantly clear by this time that we have our own BS to deal with. But man, so do they.

In fact, their BS seems so out of the ordinary that regardless of what kind of a chiropractor you are or where you went to school, it's almost as if people come from another planet. The things that people believe, the things that dictate their behaviors and determine their results are not only prevalent but are the causal reasons the health of our world is spiraling downward so quickly.

But it's not their fault. Just like us, they had mothers, fathers, teachers and preachers that instilled these beliefs within them. They bought into them and man, are they paying the price. They've been sold these beliefs by people and companies like Big Pharm which banks on its ability to sell them an idea.

Ask your doctor if the purple pill, the green pill, the yellow pill or the blue pill is best for you.

They've sold people the idea that you're raised in a medicine cabinet. They've sold the idea that you need a doctor, that your child needs a pediatrician and that birth is a disease they need to be in a hospital for.

Look, opinions aside, right or wrong is not the issue. This is what's formed the beliefs of the people who live in your community and walk into your practice. The chiropractor who spends the time and invests in the training to identify and understand exactly what their beliefs are, where they come from, what actions those beliefs compel and what results are created as an effect of those beliefs- *that chiropractor* is the one who can now clearly identify the gap between the wants and the needs.

This is the chiropractor who closes the gap, eases into the conversation, builds value based upon something much bigger than what they thought was true before, and ends up with the practice of their dreams, one based on helping people get the results of their dreams.

The prevalence of social media has brought out some of the best and some of the worst elements of our profession. The one way that you do *not* influence someone's belief system is by attacking them.

You did what to your child? You've vaccinated your child? Don't you know? Are you an idiot? Do you really think that putting a little bit of mercury in the bloodstream is good for them? Do you really think you have those headaches because you don't have enough Tylenol® in your bloodstream? Don't you know that a fever is good for you?

Making people wrong, attacking someone's belief system- even if it's completely wrong- will NEVER advance you, us, or our ability to save the community and the world. What will is understanding their beliefs and then skillfully and socratically have *them* realize the truth, just like we did with our chiro BS.

How's that working for you? *Huh. Never thought about it. Not good.* Well, have you ever thought about...? It's not a forced process as you'll learn in the upcoming chapters. Their BS is just the same as yours. Different flavor, but their ability to understand it and then embrace new belief systems that empower them to make different choices and get different results is what this is all about.

The hardest thing that you do as a chiropractor is spend your entire career trying to convince people to do something differently. Psychologists call this behavior modification. *You need to stop doing this, you need to sleep on this pillow, you to be here three times a week, you need to understand the value of subluxation, you need to get adjusted three times, and you tell all your friends.*

We are constantly striving to change people's behaviors. But the problem is, when you look at your triangle, behaviors are at the top. It's in the middle that's a cause to the behavior. If you want people to come in once a week for the rest of their life to have their nervous system checked along with their family, they have to believe the same thing you believe: that your life is better lived without nerve interference or whatever it is for you.

That's the answer. Not trying to force their behavior. Not trying to get your CA to constantly discipline them to come in. Not making it so affordable it's ridiculous. Not by opening up your hours. You can always be there and serve the whole world by simply getting them to realize the value and that life is better lived through an optimally functioning nervous system than it is without.

I get it, it's easy, it's affordable and I'm in. It's easy, but first you have to completely understand how to *unwire* and *rewire* their belief systems. Shall we?

9 I FEEL FINE

Many times I do agree that symptoms suck. However, when you look at the belief system that drives the behavior of the people who live in your community and the people that you seek to serve, there's a dramatic difference between not wanting to be sick and not wanting to feel bad and knowing what that difference actually means.

"WHILE OTHER PROFESSIONS ARE CONCERNED WITH CHANGING THE ENVIRONMENT TO SUIT THE *WEAKENED* BODY, CHIROPRACTIC IS CONCERNED WITH *STRENGTHENING* THE BODY TO SUIT THE ENVIRONMENT."

-B.J PALMER

This one doesn't necessarily need an explanation, but let's dig in deeper anyway.

One of the prevailing beliefs in society today is that if you don't have any pain and you don't have any symptoms, you're healthy. And the medical profession, for the most part, has furthered that belief. They've deepened it. They've confirmed it. Because of this, our beliefs and their beliefs are not only miles apart, they actually contradict each other. Not a great way to start a relationship.

It's critical to not point fingers and tell them they're wrong. Instead, you need to understand where they come from. They believe that if they have symptoms, if they have pain and the pain is severe or lasts long enough, then they've got to do something about that.

Maybe they go meditate. Maybe they go get a massage. Maybe they go to the chiropractor. Maybe they take some drugs. Maybe they have surgery. Whatever it is, they've got to treat those symptoms and they're going to believe Google or the medical doctor or whoever is in a position of authority at the time.

The other aspect of this, is that when they do get their treatment (and I'm using that word *specifically* because I don't believe it belongs in the chiropractic lexicon) they believe that as soon as they feel better they *are* better. We know better, but they have a belief system where feeling bad means you're sick. If you feel bad enough, you need to go get treatment for it. When you feel better, you're better.

They believe that drugs heal. They believe that drugs somehow get in the system, go find the one injured or sick cell and then heal the body, while we believe the body heals itself. These are two very contradictory ideas we must clarify for them, without making them wrong. You must understand this: we can't judge them and we can't make them wrong. We've got to understand that this is where they are. This is what they believe.

What type of questions can I ask Mary so that she shifts her beliefs to align with what I believe?

I don't believe that a cast on a broken arm heals the arm. I believe it supports the arm while the body heals itself. I don't believe that an antibiotic heals the body. I believe that it may hold something at bay and may be necessary at times, but I understand that the body is what actually heals us. If you give an antibody to a cadaver, nothing is going to happen.

I believe that the body heals itself. They believe that drugs heal. Very different. If we don't come together on that, there is no conversation.

Look, here's what they believe.

They believe that being sick is normal because everyone is sick. Being overweight is normal because everyone is overweight. Eating crap is normal because everyone eats crap. They believe their kids are supposed to have normal sicknesses. They believe in normal headaches. They believe that high blood pressure, high cholesterol and diabetes is normal because it's common. And that Big Pharm is always backing them up, confirming that what they believe is the right thing. It's good marketing. The question is, what are you and I going to do about it?

As I said in the intro, if we choose to attack them and make them wrong on a Facebook post, on Facebook Live, one on one, at a public forum, or in a discussion and we bitch and moan about medicine, say that drugs are bad and medical doctors are evil and everyone else is wrong, people won't open their arms. They'll close them if you attack their beliefs.

What if you did that about their spirituality, even if you had a contrary spiritual belief? If you truly wanted to convert someone to another belief, say from Atheism to Christianity, are you going to go in and make them feel stupid for believing that there is no God? Are you going to go in and attack their position? Well, the answer is yes- a lot of people do that. And how's that working for them?

How's it working for the dude standing on a literal soapbox in downtown San Diego on a Friday night, screaming through a megaphone that sinners are condemned to hell, Jesus Saves, and to repent now or die while people are out to dinner? How effective is that guy? How many people has that man saved for the Kingdom of God? I don't know, but I'm guessing... none.

How effective is the youth pastor that goes down and reaches out to people in need and shares a story? Asks them about what's going on and then gets permission to paint a picture of something that could be better than it is? How effective are they? Very effective. It's how things are spread throughout the world.

See, we attack people for having these beliefs. The beliefs are, in my opinion, wrong. They're simply not true. They're bullshit beliefs, but the people aren't wrong for having them. It's my responsibility to honor their belief, meet them where they are and then master the process of bringing them over toward me as I walk toward them.

That's the process of getting their *wants* to become their *needs*. That's the process of cause and effect. That's the process of communicating the truth, raising perceived value, giving them car*ing* plans and BEing Epic. That's the process. But it starts with YOU. It starts with understanding where these beliefs come from and what results are caused by the actions they take.

If people believe they feel well and don't have pain, what actions are they going to take? They're not coming to see you. They feel good! That's what their mom told them. That's what their pediatrician told them. That's what their high school health class teacher taught them. You're telling them they're not fine, and it doesn't make any sense to them. What kind of results are they going to have then? Well, you see a lot of people walk around who are "healthy" but have cancer or die of a heart attack the next day.

If people believe that when they have pain, they need to treat the pain and when the pain is gone they feel better, then what actions are they going to take? They're going to come to you when they have pain and you're going to treat the pain, drug free. That's awesome and it's better than Advil but you still treat the pain. They still believe that when they feel better, they are better.

Regardless of the care plan you put them on, that belief is still going to compel them. They don't have a choice. It's going to compel them to say, *hey I appreciate it, but I really do feel great. I'll call you when it hurts again* and because of our wonderful loving nature and our desire to be liked and respected, you'll say, *that's perfect. My patients love me and they'll come back later.* But here's the thing: they just went home with the same problem they left with, minus the pain.

If they believe (which they do) that drugs heal and then we say, *hey you don't need drugs.* Well, you're contradicting their belief and they feel like they're being attacked because none of it makes any sense yet. We've got to ask them questions and be Socratic in order to get them to expose their own limiting beliefs. And by the way, they don't say, *oh I get it now!*

I love chiropractors that say, *oh they get it, they definitely get it.* What they mean is that they get the Big Idea. They get the Big Idea and all of us say, *oh my gosh they get it!* Chiropractors don't "get it." Very few of us "get it." A patient might begin "getting it" but their belief system has to be nurtured their entire life. Because even if *you* think they get it, once they leave your practice they're going to turn on the TV and they're going to see 20 drug ads and hear it on the radio and go straight to their medicine cabinets.

Do you understand? This is a process that you and I need and will continue to break down. Once we've identified our own beliefs, our new actions and our results, then and only then we can really take a look at theirs. Now we're cooking with fuel, baby.

Now we've got gas on the fire because now we can illuminate the truth and get what we want, which is what they need. Everyone wins.

10 CAN YOU CRACK MY BACK

> "WHEN WE DON'T CLEARLY DEFINE OURSELVES, SOCIETY WILL DO IT FOR US."
>
> *-DR. DAVID JACKSON*

Like myself, I'm sure you find it interesting that chiropractic was predicated and founded upon a deaf janitor who got his hearing back. Today, it's looked at as a back-pain profession.

The two couldn't be more unrelated, other than the fact that they both involve the spine. Regardless of your philosophical connotations or what the school you graduated from taught you, it should be no surprise to any of us that currently, chiropractors are looked upon as "back doctors". Not even "real" doctors, but the people you go to when your back hurts.

One of the prevalent belief systems that the people in your practice, in your community and that most future prospects believe, is that chiropractors are limited to problems of the back.

Think about that for a minute.

If someone has back pain and happen to know a little about chiropractic because their beliefs are based upon a friend who got results or they met a chiropractor at a spinal screening or they saw a chiropractor adjust a player during an NFL game or during the Olympics and somehow, they now have a belief system that says, *chiropractors are back doctors and I've got a back problem so I'm going to see one to get that problem taken care of.*

It's not that the belief system isn't true, but it completely limits their perspective and it also limits yours because you probably have that belief system as well. Even though people come into a chiropractic office knowing very little of what to actually expect, what they anticipate is that you're going to crack their back (I despise using that phrase) and somehow, they're miraculously going to feel better.

Let's go back to what people want.

They want to feel better, yesterday, and they want someone else to pay for it. Unless they have previous knowledge, most people walk into your practice with this belief: *my back went out yesterday. I don't know what caused it, but it hurts right here, and I need you to put it back in.*

As if it's just an event. As if it's not a process.

Contrast that with how they believe an orthodontist changes the alignment of teeth. They know it takes a lot of time, years, and a lot of visits, and they know it's going to cost them somewhere between three to five thousand dollars.

Because we've done a miserable job of communicating our value through any kind of marketing effort or any kind of a branding awareness, they believe that if their back hurts they can go to a chiropractor to get their back *cracked* and then they will leave feeling all better. They'll think they don't need to continue.

While that sounds like a nice luxury, those belief systems drive the people who come in seeking back pain relief and the majority of chiropractors in our profession give them exactly what they want. They assess the area of the spine that hurts, they X-ray the area that hurts, they twist and pull on the side that hurts. Then they ask the patient if the area still hurts and if the answer is yes, they'll see them again. If it's no, they'll ask to see them one or two more times to "maintain it" and then tell them to come back if it ever hurts again. We can't blame the patients, we can't blame the community for feeling this way.

What we *can* do is change their perspective.

Not by attacking them, but by getting them to think differently. Years ago, a good friend of mine, who is a world champion big wave surfer, came and spoke at one of our trainings in front of a couple hundred chiropractors. There was one video he showed that made me freeze on a particular frame. I asked him: *wait a minute, what's happening right there?* He looked at me and said, *what do you mean what's happening? I'm about to take the wave?*

This is the wave that won him the Double XXL Big Wave Surfing Championship that year. It was a huge, nasty, monstrous wave at Mavericks, which is a treacherous break up in northern California. In this picture, there were about 12 guys who were either courageous enough (or dumb enough) to be in this competition, and eleven of them were what we call "scrapping" which means they were paddling for their lives to get over the wave before it crashed on them.

Only one of them was actually paddling *into* the waves, ready to drop in on the wave that won him the Big Wave of the Year award. I saw that and said, *what's the deal here? Why are they all paddling away from the wave and you're the only one going a different way and taking off on it?* He looked at me and said, *well that's because I always stay five to ten feet outside.*

That hit me. It hit the whole group.

Staying five to ten feet outside meant that he was unique. He was different. We're going to get into some of this in Chapter 15 as well. But when our population thinks you can only go one way or only do one thing, you've got to ease them into a different system of beliefs regarding what you're capable of, what the products are and what your skill set is. Not just with your current patients, but also in your marketing and your branding. We can't continue to put seventeen danger signals and lightning bolts on all of our advertising, all of our marketing, all of our posters and make everything about back pain.

Some will say that's what chiropractic is good at, and they're right. We are good at it, but it's not what we're best at. Just because we're good at it doesn't mean we should limit ourselves to *just* that. If you want to, that's cool. Again, there's no judgment here. But if we continue to foster the belief that chiropractors are back doctors, then it's no wonder that people want to go to the crack house and leave a couple of visits later once they've had their fix.

You might think that we as a profession and you as an individual just have to deal with it, but you're here in the middle of this book, still reading because you want something different.

You want to be 5 - 10 feet outside of the competition.

I'm going to show you how to enter that conversation. How to ask them a few simple questions so they start believing that their back is not the problem. That you're not a doctor, you're a nervous system specialist. That no one's ever checked their nervous system before.

We're going to help you reposition the conversation so that this belief doesn't hold them or you back any more.

11 IT'S NOT MY RESPONSIBILITY

"THERE'S AN EXPIRY DATE ON BLAMING YOUR PARENTS FOR STEERING YOU IN THE WRONG DIRECTION; THE MOMENT YOU ARE OLD ENOUGH TO TAKE THE WHEEL, THE RESPONSIBILITY LIES WITH YOU."

-J.K ROWLING

You and I both know that when we think about the healthcare system, the majority of chiropractors would redefine it more accurately as a sick care system. It's starting to change, but it's a bit like turning around the Titanic. It's a long journey ahead. Health care today is still looked upon as something that solely requires medical attention and you go to a "health care provider" even though it really is about sickness.

The challenge that leaves us with is a lack of general responsibility. But think about where that belief system comes from. *My insurance will pay for that,* or *I don't know what happened to me, I just got sick,* or *someone else should take care of me.* Where do these concepts even come from? We're all born to be responsible for ourselves and our own actions, but somewhere along the line that belief system completely shifts.

It stems from the fact that medicine took over the body as its domain. It said, *hey we take care of anything and everything that happens with the body,* so people said, *oh okay* and willingly gave up control and responsibility of their health to the system.

They not only gave up their control, but they gave up on the belief that their body is even their own. Think about the birthing process. In so many parts of the world, it's a natural process that happens at home or in a birthing center or out in a field and has been happening for thousands of years. But in America, it's insane the amount of pressure and skepticism you get if you want to give birth at home. People say, *are you crazy? You could have died!* Or, *where's the evidence to support that it's better to birth from home?* The sad thing is, people don't want evidence.

They have this belief system that's not true but has been handed down to them regardless. Ultimately, you've got a community full of people that aren't used to taking responsibility for their own health because when it breaks, they'll go get it fixed and someone else will simply pay for that.

What does that look like when it shows up in your practice? Well, it looks like a lot of work. It looks like a lot of trouble because people don't want to take responsibility for a lifestyle that leaves them with Phase 2 degeneration and a nervous system in serious distress. They just think they have a back problem, because that is what they've been trained to think. They expect someone else to pay for it. These are all things that are part of their belief system, their actions, and their results because they gave up on taking responsibility for their bodies.

But they're taking it back. The tide is changing. People have moved away from this belief system. A lot of that is based purely upon the availability of information on the Internet. It's changed how and what people believe.

However, this is still by and large the predominant thought.

What does that mean for you as a chiropractor who seeks to move people toward a new idea of their body? How will you show them that their families are so much better with you in it, that their experience in life is going to be optimized because they are under continuous lifetime chiropractic care with you? How do you change that? How do you get them to reassess responsibility? Well interestingly enough, it's already happening for you, and one of the things we're going to talk about in Part 3 is the idea of comparing and contrasting.

Maybe you've heard this metaphor before, but I want you to think about this. A lot of people go to a grocery store like Whole Foods because it has an organic section. They know the organic produce and meats are two to three times more expensive, and often times you get less for your money. It's nicknamed "Whole Wallet" for a reason. You get one bag for $100 versus going to another grocery store chain to get four bags for $70. It's a big difference but people willingly line up to pay the difference.

When they go to the regular grocery store, they don't segment off the organic food and say, *hey can you bill this to my third party?* They don't say, *wait I want a discount on this because it's good for me and it's not my fault that I'm sick and I need this.* They pay willingly, because over a long process of time they've shifted their beliefs to incorporate the notion that chemicals and pesticides aren't good for them.

Think about that for a minute.

Is their belief based upon the fact that they have some direct experience of feeling worse from eating nonorganic produce? No, they're doing it based upon an *idea.* They are taking back their responsibility based upon an idea, and the idea is simply that food is better off without pesticides sprayed all over it. So, they spend more money because it's good for them and their families.

Kind of sounds like, *life's better without interference, so I'll spend some money and invest in my family chiropractic care.* But you still have to give them a reason to get past the idea that insurance is the way to go. Because if you don't get them past that idea and give them a good reason as to why the organic food is not covered by insurance and is therefore little bit more expensive, then you're going to be on the receiving end of *no,* or *let me think about it,* every single time.

The issue of people not taking responsibility for their viewpoints can be solved by shifting their points of view so they begin to accept responsibility. Get them to see that it's not the past that matters, it's the future. It's for the things they want. Remember how in the very beginning of this book we said the pain, their primary symptom, isn't why they're in your office? They're there because they lost something, or they don't think they're going to be able to get something they really want.

This is where responsibility comes in. If they really want that vacation, if they really want to take their grandkids to Machu Picchu and keep up with them, then they've got to take responsibility for their health. If they really want to access their potential as you describe it to them, you need to help them nurture a belief system they actually place value in, one that they actually want.

Don't get stuck in what it *has* been. The biggest and easiest example of this is when people convert from insurance to cash. There's so much fear around it. There's always some challenge around it because you're making a massive change in your practice. But having gone through it and having helped hundreds of chiropractors through it, I'll share some advice.

First piece of advice: **it all begins with your mindset.**

It begins with you and your team's mindset about the value you actually deliver. You have to look at it as your responsibility to give them the best value for the best fee, which can only happen by eliminating the middleman. So, you're going to build up your own value. Because when they come in and say, *hey it's not really my responsibility* (based on their current belief system) you can't go on the attack and say, *come on, you don't ask Blue Shield to pay for your groceries do you?*

That's an idea for *you*. What you've got to do is build up the idea that it's their responsibility to care about being healthy, not just care about being sick. See, they understand they've never been in a health care *process,* but that's what the world is moving toward. You've got to identify yourself as much as you can outside of the sick care environment and into the health care environment.

They've already established that they're responsible for their health, but they still think that everyone else is responsible for their sickness. They haven't defined it in those words, but they know that. When you help them understand that and position yourself on the side of health, that is a *winning* position.

One last note before we move on to the next chapter: don't think you can go cash just yet. It's a process. Get help. Don't reinvent the wheel. Don't try to do it yourself without any support or guidance. Make sure you're in a community full of people who have gone through this process and can support you as you go through it. That's one of the reasons I'm so damn proud of our Epic Practice Community. They have done this over and over again and they have been freed from insurance. Not everyone (they don't all want it) but they've been freed of their dependence upon insurance.

If you depend upon insurance and insurance goes away, you don't want to go away too.

12 I CAN'T AFFORD IT

"I BET YOU GIVE A GOOD MASSAGE..."

-MODERN MAN

Many people who show up to your practice for the first time view chiropractic as an absolute luxury, not a necessity. When you check yourself and your belief system on that, its pretty easy to do.

How often do you yourself get checked? How often do you check your family? That's easy: they're there, you're there. It might not be as easy for you, but it's certainly easy for your family. It doesn't cost any money. It only takes a few minutes.

But how committed are you to the idea? If you have a problem with this idea, don't judge it- just put a stake in the ground and go back to Chapter 1 if you need to start the process over again.

If you look at chiropractic as a luxury, then you will communicate it as a luxury.

A luxury is something you want, but probably can't afford. Even though it'd be nice to have, it's something that's thought of as too expensive or out of reach. BUT if someone gave it to you, you'd take it.

The challenge then, is dealing with someone who has insurance and gives you the answer, *oh yeah, my insurance will pay for it, or yeah, I'll give it a shot. That's their commitment to their care plan.* They think, *the economy is good right now, my job is great, or I've got plenty of time to give it a shot.*

Then their insurance changes, the economy changes, it's Christmas time and they're buying presents for the kids or going on vacation and all of the sudden, your practice suffers because they still hold the viewpoint that chiropractic is a luxury, when in essence it is absolutely not.

Chiropractic is a necessity. It's a necessity for anyone who wants to live the best life they can and reach their optimal potential without interference.

It's not a necessity for people who don't want that.

Most people don't actually value their health, but those who do go through a process of learning exactly what that is. They reassign what they believe to be true and begin to view chiropractic in a completely different light.

All of this is based upon your communication skills. Almost everyone, unless they've been referred or have been to chiropractors before, shows up and views it as a luxury. The sooner you can have them view chiropractic as an absolute necessity, the better.

This is critical. In fact, it's the single most important thing you can do when they get there. It's game, set, match.

Not only will they convert their beliefs, but they will convert into a great patient who understands the lifestyle you are facilitating for them. They will understand how being face down on your table will positively affect them and their families for the rest of their lives.

They won't resort to saying, *times are a little bit rough right now so we're going to cut you out before we cut out our cable TV* or *someone got laid off so we're going to quit chiropractic care but we're going to still go to Disney World®*.

That is the difference between a luxury and a necessity. A lot of people view you like they view getting a massage. Some people do view it as the same thing, which is interesting. Isn't an hour massage at a hotel or resort about $120 an hour? Isn't it $60 - $80 at a normal massage place? It's that price for an hour because they are selling time for money.

Here we are giving an adjustment in two minutes and charging $40 to $70 dollars for a visit. What's the difference? Are we just better at business? Are we shysters? Are we ripping people off?

No, there's a difference in value.

Several times throughout this book we've touched on the notion that value is communicated. In Chapter 15 when we talk about how to raise the perception of value, you're going to see how this process can make anyone who thinks chiropractic is a luxury change their belief systems to now view it as a necessity. You can raise the perception of what things are worth to them in 10 different ways. This will be a game changer for you.

Chiropractic is a luxury for the people who don't really care and don't really understand the value and the benefit of living a life through an optimally functioning nervous system.

Chiropractic is an absolute necessity for people who understand the value and the benefit of living a life through an optimally functioning nervous system.

You will be able to communicate this necessity to them through the process I'm about to share with you. You'll know how to communicate the truth, and that truth will create Epic impact.

PART 3

THE TRUTH

"CHIROPRACTIC IS DIFFERENT NOT BECAUSE OF WHAT WE THINK, BUT BECAUSE OF HOW WE THINK."

-REGGIE GOLD

This is where the rubber meets the road. It's what you've been waiting for. It's what the profession needs. It's what saved my life and built the Epic Life that I now live. It's the same truth that has helped me help thousands of chiropractors like you live an Epic Life through building their own Epic Practice. The truth is simple, yet its impact is profound.

We begin by understanding our own truths, our own beliefs, the actions we take and the results that we get. Then we compare them to the truths of the people in our communities we choose to serve. Measuring that gap and understanding how far away they are brings us to this moment: closing the gap through the art of communication.

Communication is an intrinsic form of connectivity. Our connection in chiropractic has been sterile. It's been planned. It's been rehearsed. While that worked ten years ago, people today crave real, raw, authentic communication.

They want to do business with someone they can trust their lives and the lives of their family with. They want people who are steeped in honesty. They want people who will tell them the truth even if it hurts, but do so with love, compassion and kindness.

The truth about chiropractic through your eyes is ready to be received, and when you develop the skills to deliver it, it will be received with open arms.

There are 9 "Gears" that drive an Epic practice. All 9 are absolutely vital to crush it in practice and none of them are optional. ALL of them are required. And communication, in my opinion, is the second most important Gear out of the 9. It's second because the most important Gear of all is our own mindset, which we've been working on in Part 1 and in Part 2.

Once we have our mindset focused on the vision, the goals, the purpose, the processes and everything that will drive our actions, it's time to take our mindset and speak it into existence. Communication isn't just one-on-one, it's also one-on-many. You must learn how to communicate in a way that allows the information and the value to transfer from one person to another, whether it be to their spouse, their co-workers and so on.

Not just for referrals, but for the purpose of support.

The truth carries a massive amount of weight in the world today. The future belongs to the people who are courageous enough to define it, clarify it and stick to it. Our truth is simple. Our truth is sacred. I'm going to share exactly what mine is with you, but you must come up with a truth of your own. You will share your version, your own authentic identity that will make people seek you out and desire to have the life they've always dreamed about, and the health they all deserve.

13 CAUSE & EFFECT

"A + B = C"

-MATH

We are governed by the laws of cause and effect. Many will try to fight them. Most will die trying. The reality is those that embrace the cause and focus on it will amplify the effect that they're looking for.

It's such an important concept that chiropractic has been founded on as a profession. It doesn't look toward the effect or concern itself with the treatment of diseases or symptoms. Instead, we take a very different approach and *seek* the cause. The cause dates back to a neural function disturbance that took place in 1895.

Yes, we have progressed and yes, technology has evolved, but the dramatic difference between the chiropractic profession and everything else is that we understand the process of cause and effect within the human body, and we actually practice the *process*.

We've talked in Part 1 and Part 2 about the differences between our beliefs and their beliefs, our behaviors and their behavior, and our results and their results. But now it's time for you to make it real in your practice. Take a piece of paper and draw a big triangle. Take another piece of paper and draw the same triangle. Label the first triangle "Us" and the second triangle "Them". Yes, it is Us vs. Them for the time being.

The "Us" Triangle: Chiro Kids

What are the results that your family has? If you don't have a family yet, what are general results that a typical family under chiropractic care might have? Let's be specific.

Say you visited a successful family and wellness-based practice that's not insurance dependent. What do you see when you look at the families and children waiting to get adjusted? On average, they're not perfect but look at the children of most chiropractors. What is the result?

They're not perfect, but the overwhelming result is that they are typically healthier than average. They're intelligent. They're articulate. They're compassionate. They're aware. They excel at sports. They excel in school. They don't get sick nearly as often as other kids. They radiate health. And remember, this isn't an all-encompassing idea. My kids have been sick before but man, not compared to the rest of the world.

The "Them" Triangle: Kids Without Chiro Care

What is the result on the other piece of paper? What are the typical results of the children in your community who aren't under chiropractic care? They're sick. They're overweight. They have diabetes. They may be bullied. They may be bullies. They suffer from anxiety, depression and an astounding number are somewhere on the spectrum. The result is that they're disconnected.

Let's go back to our current triangle: our beliefs, our behaviors, our results. Now let's look at the actions. What does the average chiropractic family and the average chiropractic kid do and not do? For starters, they get adjusted. They don't take a lot of drugs, if any. They may have been born at home. They are spoken to with respect. They are taught respect. They watch less TV than the majority of kids. They play less video games. They get outside more. They eat organic foods. They talk about positive things because their parents have raised them in a positive environment. They expect a lot out of themselves and a lot out of each other.

What does the average child do? They watch dozens of hours of TV a week. They eat crappy food. They are raised in a medicine cabinet. They go to the doctor often. They get all of the vaccinations. They don't get adjusted. They don't play outside because they're playing video games.

There's a big difference. Let's go back to "Us". Why? What beliefs do parents of chiropractic kids have that compels those behaviors?

We believe that the body is designed to be well and to heal when it's not. We believe that the nervous system is in charge and that interference to the nervous system, regardless of how minor, isn't a good thing. We believe that subluxation causes interference (play along if you don't). We believe that children should eat good, nourishing food and that they should limit their exposure to all of the BS in the world that stems from TV and other people's agendas.

We believe that drugs don't heal the body, so we don't take them unless it's absolutely necessary. We believe in self responsibility and teaching that to our children. We believe in showing kindness and compassion. Chiropractors aren't perfect, but this is what most of us believe.

Those beliefs predict and compel those behaviors, and we end up with pretty frickin' bad ass kids.

What about the parents on the "Them" side. What do they believe? What do the parents believe? What do they instill within them? Again, they believe that sickness is normal. They believe that health comes in a pill or potion and exists inside their medicine cabinet. They believe that if the kids feel fine, no harm no foul, they're good. They believe that if kids are sick they go to the doctor and take something to get rid of it. They believe they need all the vaccinations and that it's a good thing for them- that it's healthy. They believe that the pediatrician is the go-to resource for raising a healthy child. They believe that food, although it matters, isn't that important because they're just kids. These beliefs (and many more) dictate their behaviors and result in less healthy and happy lifestyles for their children.

I just went through this exercise and shared my truth. Now it's your turn to take a few minutes and do the exercise yourself, and then answer this question: how dramatically different are these two triangles? When we think about the process of living in cause and effect, what is the difference? How far apart would you have to move them for the literal distance between them to make metaphorical sense?

How large is the gap? How big is it? It's frickin' huge. When we look at that gap, the challenge we face seems insurmountable. It seems nearly impossible. And for some, it is. Remember: everyone deserves chiropractic care, but not everyone wants chiropractic care.

The Coast Guard understands this concept and bases their rescue strategy around it. The Coast Guard has one critical rule when they come upon a ship in distress. Say there are 25 people on the ship and there's only four officers in a helicopter. What are they going to do? All 25 people are treading water trying not to drown. It's freezing cold. These Coast Guard officers understand this concept I'm talking about. They understand the struggle that happens in the water, so their rule is to save those who swim towards them first.

We don't have time to go after the people that don't believe us, the people that want you to convince them. It's not your job to do so. It's your job to open up their minds to new possibilities, new pathways and new ideas so they can adopt new beliefs. And if that new belief leads them to value their potential and their possibility, then you've got a deal. Do it right and you potentially have a lifetime patient in front of you.

Everyone deserves chiropractic care but not everyone wants it.

When that gap is overwhelming because it's so large, you're communicating to the wrong audience. When that gap seems like you will never be able to close it, your brand message is off.

Like so many chiropractors, it may be that you're in the process of converting from a pain-based practice to a family and wellness-based practice, and you're stuck in the middle. You're in that stretch where you're pulled in both directions. You have to hold on to the pain-based patients because those are the people paying the bills, but you want a wellness-based practice. I understand, Doc. I have been in that place many times and I've helped thousands of people through it.

But ironically, that stretch is what hurts you the most because the longer you hold on to both, your marketing and your communication is still pain-based. You're still asking everyone at every visit, *how are you feeling? Where does it hurt?* But at the same time, you're saying, *we don't really function on feeling because we're here to talk about your function instead,* etc. Now you're confused, they're confused, everyone's confused and no one knows what to think.

Look at the two triangles. Start redirecting your communication to your ideal intelligent patients, the people you really want to serve, the people that are a little bit closer together in the gap. You're not going to find them right next to each other. That gap will be there. But man, make sure it's not the frickin' Grand

Canyon. Make sure it's something you have the energy, the time and the skill set to narrow and close. When you look at those wants to feel better yesterday and have someone pay for it, when you look at the needs of functioning better from this day forward, assess how big that gap is and then put a stake in the ground.

What I mean by that is put a frickin' stake in the ground where you stand right now, today. I mean a literal stake. And don't judge it. Don't shame yourself. Don't weep over it. Don't blame anybody. It doesn't matter where your practice is at right now. What matters is where it's going to be tomorrow, a year from now and where it's going to be five years after that. However, you'll never know until you drive a stake in the ground. Until you say, *this is where I am NOW.*

It's called accepting reality.

And listen, reality can suck but your response to it doesn't have to. Put a stake in the ground. Look ahead, find out where you want to go and focus on that.

The reason a rear-view mirror in a car is so small compared to the windshield is because you only need to look back to make sure nothing's going to hurt you from behind. But ahead of you is the future. Looking out of the window is the focus. That's how you begin to close that gap. You have to become skilled at using these strategies to move people forward, *into* the value of what you have to offer them.

And the best way to do that is by communicating the truth.

14 PART 1
COMMUNICATING THE TRUTH

"THE TRUTH WILL DO."

-DR. DAVID JACKSON

It's time to dig in, Doc. Make sure you've got your pen and journal ready because we're going to talk about the **5 Levels of BE** you need to understand in order to communicate the truth and do so effectively.

1. BE AUTHENTIC

Now that sounds like it goes without saying, but the majority of chiropractors have adopted other people's images, other people's personalities and other people's success processes and attempted to make them their own. I've traveled the highways and byways and I can't tell you how many times I've seen mission statements on walls (meant to signify their personal mission) that end up being carbon copies taken directly from someone else, because they haven't established what their own authentic missions mean to them. I see the same thing with tag-lines, brands and scripts, with marketing and with communication in general.

Doc, it's critical in society today to be 100% authentic. We are surrounded by BS and we're sick of it. People need authenticity and they demand it. There's immense freedom in being authentic. This is your opportunity to embrace every flaw that you have.

It doesn't mean you excuse them away and if you're not good at something say, *that's just how I am.* I'm talking about an idea of "done beats perfect". Nobody wants Hollywood, nobody wants polished anymore, they want something real. They want raw. They want **you**. If you're a driver personality[1], then drive away. You have to be conscientious of the amiable in your practice so you don't run them over and you might have to tone it down a bit, but you've got to be *you*.

The driver must be able to reach out at appropriate times and pull up their analytical, their amiable or their expressive personalities. If you're an analytical personality and you're all about numbers and graphs but you're talking to me as an expressive, you might bore me. But I want you to be an analytical. I just

[1] For more info on the four personality profiles, please contact help@epicimpactpress.com

want you to understand that I'm an expressive type, so tap into that part of your skill set and be authentic.

Who know how animals smell fear? So does a mother. When you want to build a pediatric family based wellness practice, a mom will be able to smell that from a mile away. If you've got a slick ad department, great Facebook marketing and a cool front desk team but you lack the authenticity of calling it like you see it and sharing your truth, they'll sniff you out in no time... and result in a low Patient Visit Average.

Our culture has gone through a revolution.

Look at it through the eyes of Hollywood, the big screen and television. For years, people were engrossed in sitcoms, dramas and soap operas. They felt so connected to them. But as society advanced, people started to realize it was just TV. It wasn't real, so they began to crave reality. So all these reality shows like Survivor and The Bachelor that showed what people were "really" like exploded in popularity. Because people want to be connected to reality. We're tired of all the gimmicks and all the sets.

We want the real stuff.

Then we discovered that reality TV wasn't real.

People started fleeing from the marketplace until other organizations like Netflix and Amazon started producing more TV that was based upon true stories, biographies and documentaries, etc. There's still plenty of drama and comedy, but the entire industry has changed because people are fed up with all of the crap. They have a hard time deciphering between what's real and what's contrived.

They don't know who to trust.

Ten years ago, when a patient walked into your office it was because they listened to your radio ad or overheard someone talking about you, but today, they've Googled your ass. They've been on your Facebook page. They know as much about you as they do about their condition because they've asked the almighty Google about that too. They've done their homework. Mothers who are looking for results for their children often know more about the condition and the situation than you do. And that's a good thing.

You've just got to be honest.

You've got to come across as authentic. The only thing that holds people back from doing so is the fact that it's in our human nature to be harder on ourselves than we should be. Our own self judgment is what holds us back. To think, *I'm not good enough. I don't deserve this. Who am I to think that* etc., is what truly limits us.

Part of being authentic is basing who you are on the things that you believe in. Hence the reason why we've been having you do the hard work. It changes who you are.

People still ask me all of the time, *how did you go from being broke to being so successful?* As if I'm going to be able to share some ten-step action plan stating how I just did things differently. Maybe I wore a different pair of shoes or I got a new poster. See that's what they look for, but what they find out is that I figured out what I believed in and stayed authentically aligned to it.

There's a process that I teach called "staying in your lane." I live in San Diego where the I-5 (one of the major freeways) goes all the way from Northern California down to the Mexican border. It's a wide freeway and yet it's always backed up. However, there's rarely any gridlock in the HOV carpool lane.

We have a lane like that in chiropractic with our name on it. It's got diamonds all over it. No one is in it and yet we keep trying to go into other people's lanes because we don't believe that what we have is enough. We don't believe that a chiropractic adjustment is enough. We believe that we always have to do more and end up focusing on other things we think are necessary or might help but ultimately end up hindering us.

Don't diverge, *converge.*

Focus the beams of light onto one target. Be authentic about that one thing you do better than anyone else. I'm not suggesting you give everything up or that you don't add anything. If that's your gig that's your gig. But I strongly encourage you to look deeply into the idea of being an honest, authentic expert in the lane of chiropractic where *you* can ride but no one else can.

Believe in yourself, regardless of your upbringing. Regardless of whether you think you truly deserve things or are just a humble servant, believe that you have something powerful in your hands. When you can transfer that through the art of communication by being authentic, people will want to have that conversation with you.

That's why being authentic comes FIRST.

You can't go to someone's seminar, take their script, implement it and expect it to work. Oh, it will work for a little while, but then you're going to burn out and people will think you're a fraud because they'll know it's not you. You'll feel it.

We get so excited when someone shares all of their strategies with us. Your pens start moving quickly, scratching down all the steps and exactly what they are. You end up thinking, *I wish I recorded that. I want to say it exactly like that. I want to report findings exactly like Dr. Jackson does.*

...No. You don't.

You want to listen to the *concepts*. This is why in Epic Practice we don't give out scripts, we teach concepts, so you can own the concept and be authentic. Because research has proven over and over again, that he or she who is the most authentic *wins*. Part of BEing authentic is allowing for the second level of BE.

2. BE DIFFERENT

Give people the sense they've never met anyone like you before. We've talked a little bit about this, but one of the concepts I utilize when I teach is what I call "the dinner conversation."

Imagine you've completed Day 1 with Mary and you've delivered your report of findings. What happens at the dinner table on day one when her spouse comes home? What happens when she talks to her friends or the people at her work? What does she tell her roommate when she comes home? There's bound to be a question:

You saw the chiropractor today, right? What'd they say?

How do you want that Day 1 conversation to go? What do you want them to say about you? That you were nice? How do you think the conversation went?

I'd love for you to write down some notes really quick. Be honest with yourself: what do you think they said at dinner? I've eavesdropped. Let me tell you what they say the majority of the time. I'll use Mary as an example once again.

Mary comes home from a typical chiropractic Day 1 and her husband asks, *how did it go?* Mary will typically say:

It was good. The office is right by where we used to go work out, so it was really convenient. The staff was nice and it was easy. I filled out the forms when I got there and then he asked me about my headaches and how long I've been having them. Then he moved my neck around, took some X-rays and said he's going to develop them tonight and he'll tell me about them tomorrow.

That's what she'll say.

Use whatever version of it you like, but that's what the majority of the conversations sound like. The better question is, what do you *want* Mary to say? Here's what I'd like Mary to say:

Hey, I forgot to tell you that I went to the chiropractor today and you know what, I have to tell you something. I've never met anyone like Dr. David or seen anything like that. When I walked in, the practice was full and it was full of families. There were kids everywhere, and there was a toy area and posters for kids. Everyone seemed so happy. The staff was super friendly and offered me tea and some organic fruit. It was such a comfortable environment and they even helped me with my paperwork.

When I sat down with Dr. David, it was obvious he had already studied all of my paper work and knew what he was talking about. He knew I had headaches, he knew how long I've had them, he knew the names, ranks and serial numbers of every doctor I've ever been to before and you know what he did? He listened to me. I mean, I know that sounds crazy, but he really listened. He asked me questions I'd never been asked before. He asked me about what everyone else had done and then he said something that really blew my mind. He said that it wasn't good for my health or his reputation to do the same thing that everyone else has done and asked me if he could do something differently. At first, I didn't understand what he was talking about, but then he talked to me about this whole other idea which I'll explain in a minute but honestly,

....it blew my mind.

I'm actually really excited to go back tomorrow because he did the scan of my nervous system and said if it turns out like he believes it will, then he will absolutely be able to help me. He'll tell me how long it's going to take, how much it's going to cost, what I have to do to get the results, he'll answer any questions I have and best of all, I can start tomorrow.

That's what I want her to say. A pretty far cry from what the normal conversation looks like. We could go through the same process during the Day 2 conversation, but on Day 1 I want them to be praying that I find that "sub-lux-tration thing" in their spine.

Let's circle back to a point I made earlier for a moment. When Mary completes the paperwork that asks her what's going on and what her health concerns are etc., don't make her repeat them again. Don't walk into the room and say, *what can I do for you Mary? What seems to be the problem?* She's just spent 15 - 20 minutes filling out the paperwork that answers that question.

Instead, walk into the room with warmth, authority and certainty, shake Mary's hand and BE Unique (and effective):

Hi, I'm Dr. David Jackson. It is an absolute pleasure to meet you and I'm so grateful that your friend and coworker Joe recommended me. We've had such great results with him and we're looking forward to having some great results with you as well. If you're a friend of Joe's, you're a friend of ours.

So, Mary, I've read through your paper. Thank you for filling that out. It sounds like you've had these nasty headaches for way too long. Six years or so. Is that correct? Mary nods.

It also looks to me like you haven't ignored them. You have been to two different doctors, an orthopedist and a physical therapist and you've actually been to TWO chiropractors before. Sounds like you've had several massages, you've tried yoga, you've taken Advil®, Tylenol®, and you've even had a Imitrex® shot. Sometimes they help, sometimes they don't. Is there anything I'm missing from your history? I know that it gets really severe at times, it happens at ___ frequency and it seems to pull on your eyes. I'm going to assume that every time you went to the doctor, they had your best intentions in mind. I don't know any of your doctors personally, but I'm going to assume that they did. But my experience tells me that they were looking for something in particular.

Listen up Doc. This is me differentiating from the rest and communicating authentically with Mary.

Mary, tell me if I'm wrong, but after looking at your history and taking into consideration what I know from past experiences, I'm guessing they were all looking for something very specific. Each and every one of them. They were each looking at a particular way to get rid of your headaches and make you feel better. The massage therapist will treat your headaches one way, the medical doctor might give you a medication or some prescription, the chiropractor will treat you in another way and so on, but they were all geared towards finding out how they could take care of your headache... and that's why you showed up in my office today.

At this point she's starting to get that curious look in her eye. Listen this is not a script, but if it resonates, understand it. BE authentic and make it your own if it resonates. Build the belief system so you can do it the first place and then have at it.

Mary, may I ask permission to go about this visit differently?

Now that, by the way, is called a pattern interrupt. No one's ever asked Mary a question like that in a healthcare provider's office before. NEVER.

So Mary listen, I'm just going to say it straight. There are two things that are of highest importance to me in this practice. The first and foremost is your help. I want to give you health, potentiality and possibility like you've never experienced before. That's number one. Number two, is my own reputation. But you know what's really cool? When I achieve number one, I achieve number two.

Again, as I was going through your paperwork I counted that you've been to two medical doctors two chiropractors, a massage therapist and have taken multiple drugs. You've been to at least six or seven different well-meaning experts who have tried to help you by treating the headaches themselves and I have to be honest with you, it sounds like they all tried a different version of a 'stickier bandaid' to solve your problem... get rid of your symptoms, your headaches.

Let me ask you a question Mary.

Now I'm going to ask this question based upon who Mary is. It's all going to be mostly relative (based on each individual) but I would say something like this:

Let me ask you a question Mary, have you ever had the flu, have you ever broken a bone or skinned a knee?

It might be a different set of questions for someone else, but I will ask her a health-related question until she says yes.

You've broken a bone, but is the bone in your arm broken today? When she tells me that it's fine now I will simply ask, *what happened?*

This is called the Socratic method and leads us to the third level of BE.

3. BE SOCRATIC

Don't tell them what happened, just keep quiet and be patient. What happened... so your arm did what? I'm not going to tell her, but I'm going to extract the words: *it healed.* Once she says it healed I'll say something like this:

So, I'm curious, did the plaster go in and glue those bones back together? Did the plaster go in and heal your body? What happened?

Pause for her answer and help if you need to, but do NOT give the answer. Wait until Mary says: *It healed.*

Exactly. The plaster held it in place, but your body healed itself. If you scrape your knee or get sick, even if you need stitches, the body is what heals, not the stitches or antibiotics. If you put stitches or Advil into a cadaver, what's going to happen? Nothing. Because life heals. See, the body heals itself. That's what it's built to do.

So, Mary, I'm curious and I bet you are as well as to why your body hasn't healed itself from these headaches. That's what it's supposed to do. It recovers from the flu, heals from a broken bone, heals from a car accident and heals from a scraped knee. I've had headaches too, but I don't have them anymore. My body healed. Yours temporarily go away, but they always come back. Does that make any sense? Does that surprise you?

And here I'll get her to say exactly what she's thinking in the moment. She'll say, *no one has ever asked me this question before.* She'll think, *this is different, I like different.* Finally, I'll pull the hope card out of my back pocket.

I don't want to reproduce things that don't work. I don't want to waste your time, I want to honor you. I'd like permission to go about this differently and do an evaluation to find out why your body is not healing properly, because your body is built and designed to function properly. I'll explain the process to you, but it certainly sounds like something is interfering with your body's ability to heal. If it's not healing optimally and I can find out what is disturbing or interfering with the healing process, then I will absolutely be able to tell what is wrong and help you fix it. How does that sound?

And Mary will say, *Doc, that sounds like the best news I've had in a long time.*

This is how you differentiate authentically. This is how you tap into the third BE in a Socratic fashion by asking questions and letting them fill in the answers. This way they anticipate a result that you want to deliver to them.

What I'm about to share with Mary is based upon my beliefs, and I've got a process now for her to identify and question her own beliefs. I've already started the process. I didn't make any of her doctors wrong, I just said I didn't want to do the same thing over and over again. That hasn't happened. What we have done is communicate with Mary in line with the third BE by Socratically asking her questions and having her call the shots. So now Mary is excited and believes in her body's ability to heal. But let me ask you a question, do I believe that? Do I believe her body is self-healing? Because this question leads us to the next level.

4. BE CERTAIN

This is where Chapters 1 through 8 all come into play, because now it's time for you to BE certain. I shared with you that I can't be certain if someone is going to feel better or not. I can't be certain of a lot of things, but here are five essential things I can be certain of. Here are five truths that pulled me out from under the hood of a car and put me back in chiropractic. Here's how I can Socratically be different and authentic with Mary and say:

Mary, the body is designed to heal. That's what it does. It breaks, and it gets better. It's self-healing. It's an amazing thing. Wouldn't you agree?

Do I believe it? Yes. Does she believe it? Yes. Has she ever thought about it before? No, because up until now she thought medicine healed. But now that I've given her examples of broken bones and the flu and medicine and the cadaver she realizes the body is self-healing. She's not placating me. She's agreeing with me because she has a new belief system that I established immediately.

Mary, the body is self-healing and I'm glad you agree with me. And what do you think controls the body? Is there one system that controls all of the others? If so, is it the big toe? Is it your left kidney? Is it your brain? What controls the entire body?

And if she guesses the heart tell her that she's close, but what controls the heart?

That's right, the brain.

So Mary, the body is self-healing, that's the way it's designed, built and structured and it heals itself through how the brain communicates. The brain communicates through a vast network called the nervous system. It communicates through the nervous system and your body heals because everything is connected through that system. From your brain to your heart, from your brain to your lungs, from your brain to the blood vessels in your head and from your brain to the nerve in the back of your eye where you feel the headaches most intensely.

See you personalize whatever they're dealing with. I'm going to say that the brain connects to all of these things much like a cell phone connects your child to the outside world. I know she has children because I've done my homework and I'm going to personalize it.

Let's say one of my three daughters borrowed the car to run an errand. It gets dark and it's raining, and all of the sudden I get a frantic call from her and I see that instead of five bars of service I only have one, so the call is garbled and broken. Just telling you this story gets my heart to beat faster. That's simply not okay is it? That lack of communication between us is now very dangerous because she might be stranded on the side of a freeway. It could literally be life or death.

Since your brain is connected to your heart, the muscles in your head, your kidneys, your immune system and your digestive system, communication is critical and you need all of the bars of service you can get. So your body is self-healing and heals the brain through the nervous system, but if it can't do that correctly because there's a disturbance to that flow, like a break in the cell signal, that's not okay.

Now Doc listen, I'm just going to call it like I see it. I'm going to tell you my authentic truth. ANY lack of communication is not ok. I was not put on earth to judge how much disturbance to a nervous system or how much disease is okay. I don't believe that anyone would choose to have any interference if they actually understood what it is. I don't want any in my life, my kid's lives or my wife's life.

So Mary, the body is self-healing, the brain controls the body through the nervous system and if you interfere with that communication whatsoever, it's not good. There's a process called subluxation, which is when your spine distorts due to stress and can twist and stretch the spinal cord and nerves which creates a different tone, like guitar strings that are too tight or too loose.

You can do some temporary fix, but that sets up a process where now the nervous system can't communicate right. All of those healing messages are disrupted to some degree and now we have a bigger problem. Does that make sense to you Mary?

She'll respond that *yes, it makes perfect sense. I've never heard it put like that before.*

So what we're going to do now, is find out if you have any interference from subluxation. I'm the best at finding these disturbances- it's what I do. If you do have any, I'm going to show them to you and talk to you about them. If I believe I can help you, I'm going to tell you exactly what your investment of time, energy and money will be and what you can expect in return. I'll answer any questions you have, and I'll get you adjusted for the first time tomorrow.

Now we've spent fifteen minutes describing this, but once you practice and master it, it's only going to take you five to seven minutes. When you can BE Authentic, when you can BE Different, BE Socratic and BE Certain, you can now BE the fifth level:

5. BE SIMPLE

I didn't get into complex neurology or complex terms to try to impress her. I'm going to get into a simple process and I'm going to use a simple tool. This is a tool I was first introduced to at a lecture by Dr. David Singer some 25 years ago. I thought it was brilliant, so

I adopted it, modified it and have used and taught it ever since.

I call it the **7 Figure Diagram.** Not because there are seven figures in it, but because it helped me build a 7-figure cash practice.

> To see this process in action so you can model it and make it your own, visit: **myepicpractice.com/7figure**

When Mary comes back on Day 2, she'll want me to find the subluxation and do my report findings with her. I can now do something most can't do: I can communicate honestly with her. I can get in her lane because her belief system is already changing. She now believes the body is self-healing, that her brain controls the nervous system, that interference is bad and that I am the best in the world at correcting it.

The only question left is, did I find it?

I use the INSiGHT™[2] system. I recommend it because you don't want to focus on bones, you want to focus on the nerves. This is hands-down the best tool in the profession that will help you know everything you need to know about the state of your patients' nervous system, helping you communicate it clearly and with certainty.

---

[2] For more information on the revolutionary INSiGHT™ System, visit www. insightcla.com

One thing I am going to say during my evaluation is this:

Okay Mary, now we're going to perform the single most important test you'll ever take in this office. It's potentially the most important test you've ever taken regarding your health.

We're going to use a very sensitive, advanced piece of equipment I am highly trained in to record the function of your nervous system. Now, this is not the part of the nervous system that tells us how you feel. This is the part of the nervous system that controls the vessels in your body, the organs, the glands, your heart, your lungs, liver, kidneys and your digestion.

We're also going to do a test that records the tone of your muscles, how much electrical circuitry is going in and how many millionths of a volt of electricity are firing through your muscles. We're going to get an overall score with this that we'll be able to compare to what's optimal. Just like you would your blood pressure, your temperature or your cholesterol. Once we have your scores tomorrow, I will define and explain them in a way that makes sense to you.

When I come back, I'm going to reiterate what we did on Day 1 (knowing that she wants me to have found the problem). I'm going to be consistent and reiterate Mary's issues so we are on the same page:

Mary, remember our conversation when I said I didn't want to be just another person on your list of past providers? I don't want you to go to the next doctor and say, "Dr. David didn't work" because that means you didn't get better and now my reputation is at stake. So, I'm not going to look for a stickier Band-Aid.

You'll notice I've already said that three or four times by now, but there's a reason for that. I'm about to reveal how important it is, and how I actually want to do things different.

You kindly gave me the permission to look and see why your body wasn't healing. We talked about how your body is self-healing and that the brain controls the entire body. Do you recall how we said the brain communicates with every cell in your body? Precisely... through your nervous system. We also discussed that if you interfere with that nervous system, even in the slightest bit, well that's bad.

We performed some high tech testing to go along with our evaluation, and I'm happy to let you know that I believe I have found the problem and I'm even happier to report that I am confident I can help you.

Let me show you what's going on.

I take her through my scans (or X-rays, test, whatever you do) and say: *this is how it everything would look if your nervous system was functioning optimally and therefor your body was working at its best.*

I explain balance, pattern, tone and core score.

Here's optimal and here's you. What do you think? Let her answer… *not good. I agree, it doesn't look good.*

That's it.

I can be simple, because that's my style. If you're more analytical, you can go a *little* more in-depth, but don't think they're necessarily analytical. If I've got an analytical personality type, I'll give them a few more details, but I'll be quick. I don't need to be a radiologist, I don't need to be a neuro specialist.

Here's what it should look like: *what do you think?* I don't tell them, I ask them what *they* think. I tell them that the results are color coded: *blue is bad, red is worse and black is extreme* to which they respond, *oh my gosh, I've got red and black all over.* I'll ask them what that means and they'll say, *well it means that I've got the interference thing like you said.* Then I'll let them know that indicates nerve disturbance in and around the area. I'll tell them they are experiencing some neurological stress, which is why their score is so unusually high.

I define or show it to them, and then I use this simple tool: the 7 Figure Diagram.

14 PART 2
THE 7 FIGURE DIAGRAM

"IF A PICTURE IS WORTH A THOUSAND WORDS, THIS WILL SAVE YOU YEARS IN YOUR CAREER."

-DR. DAVID JACKSON

When it comes to simplicity and effectiveness, there's no better educational tool than the 7 Figure Diagram. It's simple and it just makes sense.

I'll walk you through it like I'm doing it with Mary, but don't just regurgitate this as a script: you must *understand* and own the concept in order to effectively and authentically utilize it.

Let's dig into how to use this simple yet profoundly effective tool.

BRAIN-BODY

"So Mary, we talked about the fact that your body is self-healing and that your brain controls and coordinates your entire human experience: it controls your heart, lungs, sinuses, immune system, and allows you to have energy during the day and sleep well at night. We know that it does all of this through the nervous system.

FUNCTION

Since your body is self-healing, when your brain can communicate clearly through your nervous system, without any interference, your body will function optimally. We talked about living life through your nervous system, you said that that you believed it was extremely important that it functions optimally, as often as possible from this day forward, right Mary?

EASE

When every cell in your body is functioning in harmony, we have an overall state that we refer to as a state of 'ease.' It means exactly what it sounds like: your body is at ease and is working like it's supposed to. The body was created- like we talked about earlier- to be well rather than sick, right? Health is the natural state of the body and getting you to that point is our primary intent.

HEALTH

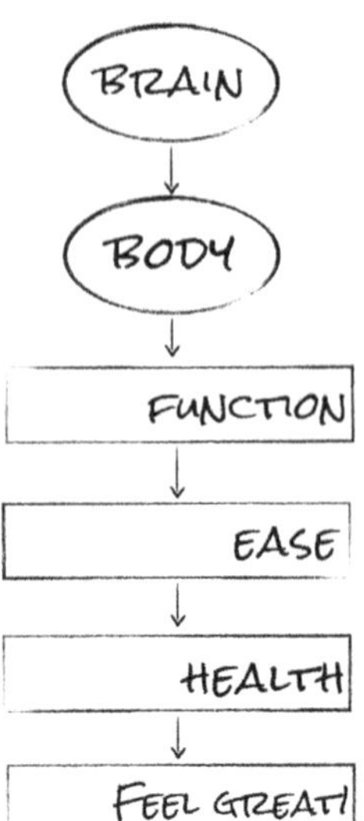

Now Mary, being in a state of optimal function leads to ease, and when it does so long enough, it means your body will be in a state of health, defined by the World Health Organization as 'A state of complete physical, mental and social well-being and not merely the absence of disease or infirmity.'[3]

FEEL GOOD

Mary, since you understand that your body is self-healing, that your brain controls the body through your nervous system and that as long as it does so without interference your body will be at ease and in a state of health. How do you think you would feel the majority of your days without interference?

(Write down the exact word Mary says as she describes how she would feel.)

Now move on to *here's the cause of your problem* and remember, her "problem" was her headaches, now it has shifted (her beliefs) to her healing.

[3] Preamble to the Constitution of WHO as adopted by the International Health Conference, New York, 19 June - 22 July 1946; signed on 22 July 1946 by the representatives of 61 States (Official Records of WHO, no. 2, p. 100) and entered into force on 7 April 1948.

NERVE DISTURBANCE

Mary, this is what your optimal, healthy body looks like. You came here looking for a solution to your headaches and we agreed that finding the *cause* would be a much better solution: the reason why hasn't your body already healed so you feel better. Remember those areas we found on your scans? They represent several subluxations: misalignments in your spine that have interfered with your nervous system. Looking at your scans again, you can see there are multiple areas where you have mild, moderate and severe areas of nerve disturbance caused by these subluxations.

MAL-FUNCTION

So Mary, what do you think happens to the body when the brain can't communicate with it optimally due to nerve disturbance? Do you think you have better function or worse function? Yes, I agree with you Mary that it would be worse. If you cut off the supply, then you're not going to have an optimal state of function. What you're going to end up with is a state of mal-function.

DIS-EASE

When a body malfunctions long enough, do you think it's going to be in a state of ease? That's absolutely right: we call that dis-ease. You can see that word is very close to disease, and if left unchecked long enough, disease sets in and you move on to the next phase.

ILL-HEALTH

Mary, I'm not saying that this is the pathway you're going to follow, but I want you to consider that this is how the body works. If left unattended long enough, dis-ease wreaks havoc on our health. Do you think you're currently in the state of health you deserve? I agree with you, definitely not. And when you get here, you no longer feel good, do you Mary? How do you feel?

(Write down exactly what she says and get her commitment to care that SHE chooses.)

BAND-AID CARE

Here's my question for you (covering the words "Feel Bad" with my hand): if we were to figure out how to get you feeling better, but you still had ill-health, dis-ease, mal-function all because of interference to your nervous system, would you actually *be* better? I agree. If we were to simply address the problem of feeling bad (what I call Band-Aid/relief care) to make you feel better and then stop, you will still be in a state of ill-health due to the nerve disturbance caused by subluxations in your spine. That's probably why the things you've tried in the past didn't work... they were directed at the symptom and not the cause.

That's not what you're looking for according to what you shared with me, right?

CAUSE VS. EFFECT

If you continued care long enough for us to help you feel better and restore your health, ease and function but the cause of the problem, the subluxation and nerve disturbance, was still there, would you be "done" with care? That's right. Until we fully address the cause of the problem, your body cannot heal and function the way in needs to and the way you deserve it to.

Mary, this leads us to the most important decision you will make in our office. I'm here to help. I work for you.

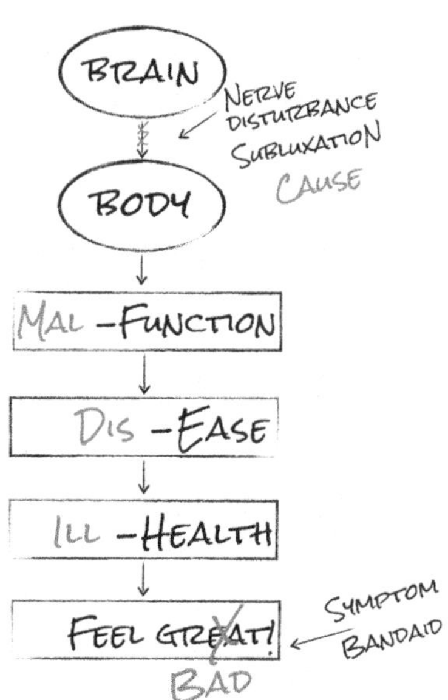

(Hand Mary the pen.)

How would you like me to help you? By doing what I can to help you feel *better* but ignoring the cause OR by setting you on a plan to *correct* the cause? Please circle which choice you want me to help you with.

(This is an immensely powerful moment when

her newfound belief system drives her decision, without being coerced or manipulated, to correct the cause!)

THE CLOSE

Mary, that's a great decision and it's a decision I'm committed to. It's a decision that my patients make again and again. And here's the best part: correcting nerve disturbance is what I do best in the world. I promise you that I will do everything in my power to work with you to help correct the nerve disturbance and identify the things that caused it to begin with. We will work together to make sure that we remove the disturbance and allow your body to work the way it's intended to.

—

Now it's time to present them with your honest recommendations, with the focus on saving their life, not saving them money.

...The Truth Will Do, Doc. Stop complicating things. All a patient wants to know is:

1. Can you help me
2. How long is it going to take
3. How much is it going to cost

The 7 Figure Diagram answers all three questions and begins to align their vision with your chiropractic vision. Remember, this is a process. It doesn't happen overnight. But if you use this tool and do so authentically and consistently, this will be the biggest game changer in your chiropractic career.

15 RAISING PERCEIVED VALUE

"IN ABSENCE OF VALUE, PRICE IS THE ONLY CONCERN."

-J.P MORGAN

I trust you're excited and can now see the absolute power of communication as it relates to building the practice of your dreams. Communication goes far beyond your ability to ask when the headaches started or how long the child has been having an ear infection: it goes into the essence of connecting with somebody.

Part of the process of connecting with others is understanding that our truth is probably not their truth, thus understanding that our belief systems and their belief systems aren't similar either. Measuring the gap and bringing the two belief systems together is one of the absolute most important elements to this process, along with understanding and respecting perception.

We all have a different perception. I'm a car guy. My father was a car guy. He drove Porsche's when I was very young and took me to the races whenever he could. I thought cars were the coolest thing in the world.

I grew up working on cars, loving cars, racing cars, and now I own some amazing cars. I find massive value in taking my car down the coast on date night with my wife and experiencing the thrill of track days racing around a Formula 1 circuit. I place this as one of my highest values in life, not for the car itself, but for the experiences it creates. Others look at a car like mine and say, *what a waste, it's just transportation.* To others it only has to be safe and reliable because that's their value system.

Neither of us are right. Neither of us are wrong. **We just have a different perception of what's important, of what's valuable.** The single most important thing you have to communicate when it comes to getting people to convert to lifetime care is perceived value. We have to understand not just what we value, but we have to find out what they value as well.

Think back to Mary with the migraine. Did she really value not having the migraine, or is what she valued her ability to be the mom that she always desired to be? There's a value there. People can easily put a dollar value on getting rid of a headache. Couple of bucks. 50 bucks. 100 bucks. Yeah, I'll get rid of my headache for that. But when you change the value process, when you increase the perception of what's valuable, they're willing to do whatever it takes.

There are 10 clearly defined processes, strategies, (tactics, if you will) that I have utilized and taught that will radically increase someone's perception of value. You shouldn't expect to implement them all, but my hope is that you choose the top three you know are going to help get things started so you can go at it with everything you have.

Some are easy. Some happen over the course of time. Others, you might be doing already but can absolutely take to a higher level. Essentially, this list of the 10 perceived values is a guide. A cheat sheet for you to determine how you can increase the value of your services, instead of lowering prices and increasing the discounts.

Because at the end of the day, I will pay for the things I value most.

Let's start with a question: what's the difference in value between a bottle of Nestlé® water and a bottle of Fiji® water? They're both similar (after all, they are water), yet Nestlé® is priced at .56¢ and Fiji is priced at $1.66. So, what's the difference in value? Is it aesthetics, clarity of the plastic, source of the water... is it the label? Or is it that one water is of higher quality and therefore the price is different?

The real difference in value is in the perception from the consumer.

When someone perceives health or taste with minimal importance in their life and all they want is a drink of water, the Nestlé® water bottle is going to be more valuable to them because it's the low-cost leader. However, if superior taste, quality and brand is more important to them, they may opt for Fiji®.

Either way, the products' "real" value is very similar, but the perception of value in the eye of the consumer is all that matters and justifies the more than 100% higher cost of one vs the other.

When the perceived value is *greater* than the exchange, people will buy. But the opposite is also true: when the perceived value is *less* than the exchange, they will not buy.

So, the only variable really, is not greater or lesser. It's the perception of the value which leads us to ask the question: *How do we better understand value, and how can we create a better "perception" of it so we can help more people?* Ultimately, you end up with two options:

Option 1: Lower the price so it falls BELOW their perceived value.

Option 2: Increase the perception of value to cross ABOVE their price threshold.

Personally, I chose option 2. The idea is to learn how to better increase the perception of value. If we are to consider the question: what's the perceived value of chiropractic care today? We could argue that it's better now than in the past because our profession is more accepted.

But I could actually argue that it's worse than before, partially *because* we are more accepted. Because we are now viewed as a commodity, the perception of our value is the lowest it's ever been.

However you view it, an untold secret to practice success lies within your ability to master the art of increasing perceived value. Listen up, because the following 10 strategies will help you do just that.

THE TOP 10 STRATEGIES TO INCREASE PERCEIVED VALUE

1. CREATE AUTHORITY, CELEBRITY, AND EXPERTISE

Disclaimer: you may think it's difficult, and you're right- it is. This is why I purposefully started off with a long game strategy.

First and foremost, why does creating and positioning yourself as an authority, celebrity, and as an expert cause people to perceive you differently? Let me ask you another question, who gets paid more for the same thing? Someone who is in authority, or someone who is a hobbyist? Someone who is a celebrity, or someone who's an amateur? Someone who's an expert, or someone who is a novice? Loaded question. What I'm driving at here, is how to understand the power of perception.

Here's a perfect example: my partner in Epic Pediatrics[4] and one of our Epic Leaders, Dr. Tony Ebel. You can look at Dr. Tony and say, *well that's a different scenario.* No, it's not.

What made him the expert in the Perfect Storm©? He did. He said he was the expert.

---

[4] For more info about the profession's leading Pediatric training program, visit: www.myepicpractice.com/epicpeds

How did he increase his authority and celebrity? He told everyone that he was the expert. Did he study and gain more expertise? Yep, and he shared it all in the form of Epic Pediatrics.

Does he go out on Facebook and talk to an audience that is congruent with his expertise? Yes. Does that build celebrity? Yes.

Does getting likes and comments on your page and getting in front of a couple dozen, or a couple hundred, or a couple *thousand* people increase your celebrity, authority, and expertise? Yes.

The answer to the question is yes, yes, yes.

There are a lot of ways to go about this, but you're the only person who can create your own authority, celebrity, and expertise. And it's not a selfish thing, it's a self-fulfilling prophecy.

Look, if I'm going to bring my kids in to see you, you better be the authority, you better be an expert, and you better have celebrity status, because I would rather pay you more money knowing that you're the best of the best, than go to someone who is not. Now, I won't buy a bottle of Nestlé® water, and in fact, I won't drink one. Is it that much worse? I don't know, and I don't care. But I'm the kind of patient that you probably want, because I have a value system that's more aligned with yours.

So how do you find people who value their health? Value ideals, value their potential and value their future more than the people who value how big their super-sized drink is? One of the ways is by creating a brand where you are the authority, the celebrity, and the expertise in your field.

Facebook allows you to do so much to raise your authority, celebrity, and expertise. At our recent Epic Accelerator training, I overheard one of our members doing a Facebook Live for his community about how he was away training with the best of the best. His audience saw that and now they perceive him as an expert. He did it in front of hundreds of people, so now the majority of his audience perceives him as a celebrity and an authority because he gained knowledge that was unattainable to anyone else outside of Epic Community.

There are so many ways to do this. You can write blogs. You can put posts together. You can author articles. There are so many small ways that you can go about this. You don't need to spend 20 hours a week doing things to create authority, celebrity and expertise. You just need to actually DO IT.

2. INCREASE YOUR FEES

Let's get this one out of the way, because you can simply increase your perceived value by increasing your fees. You may have already, or you may need to.

And I'm not only talking about adjusting fees, but let's talk about them for a moment. This one is supported by a tremendous amount of research.

I'm not talking about me, although I've done my own research at the "University of Hard Knocks" but I'm talking about actual research that's been done on *how* and *what* people value and what they'll pay for what they value. Again, this depends on what type of clientele you want to attract.

People who place a higher value on health for their own selves and for their families have very similar traits and beliefs. They are hardwired to believe that quality costs money, and that low prices indicate cheapness.

These are the kind of people who gravitate towards Option 2. But those of you who devalue your services, don't charge enough, have a low OVA and set your discounts far too high, what you're doing is choosing Option 1. You're placing the price barrier *beneath* the prospective clients' threshold, which means they are far less likely to actually say, *yes I want this.* That is the last place any business (other than a Wal-Mart) wants to be, because it is unsustainable. It is unrewarding, and research has shown that you will not get the results you want.

The other group, the people who see something of higher value, will automatically pay more because of what that cost *implies*. Now, it doesn't mean you can go from a $30 adjustment to a $300 adjustment, but you need to go from being a commodity, to being of value, and ultimately you can do this by increasing your fees.

I've studied Dr. Robert Cialdini for years. As an author, he's conducted extensive research[5] on the psychology of persuasion, perception, and how to better understand and alter the viewpoint of another human being. According to Dr. Cialdini, "in markets in which people are not completely sure of how to assess quality, they use price."

Is this chiropractic or what? People honestly have no clue how to assess quality. They may have been to a 'low price leader,' an expensive chiropractor, or anything in between. As Cialdini says, "in markets in which people are not completely sure of how to assess quality, they use price" as the stand in. Low price = low quality. High price = high quality. If you want to fill your practice with high quality people, then according to the research you should have higher priced processes, right? Your fees should be a little bit higher.

---

[5] Cialdini, Robert. *INFLUENCE AT WORK*, www.influenceatwork.com/.

This is another example I personally find very satisfying. Stanford, in a collaborative effort with Caltech, did a study on perceived value of perception by taking five different wines and conducting a taste test. Now, they actually had three wines and two of them were frauds. The two "frauds" were still wine, but not the wine they claimed was in the bottle. One was a $5 bottle of wine. Another was a $45 bottle of wine and so on, up to $90 per bottle. The participants were aware of the price, although the $90 wine rated the highest, it was actually the $5 wine.

Not surprisingly, the $5 wine rated the lowest, even though in reality it was the good stuff!

So many DC's have formed a (limited) belief that when we set our fees, we need to make them affordable. And while that can be true in a family practice, we have to make sure that the *perception* of those fees is both of quality *and* affordable.

Going back to Cialdini again, most of you do scans and use the INSiGHT System in markets in which people are not completely sure how to assess quality. You are saying (at least you should be) that this is the single most important test you will ever perform in this office, and it may be the single most important test they've ever had. Why are we saying that? Because we're driving perception of value toward the outcome of neurology instead of, *oh it hurts really bad.*

Most chiropractors increase the perception of value based upon whether or not it hurts. But as soon as it no longer hurts, the people stop coming and the chiropractors start wondering why people don't value their care anymore.

It's so flippin' obvious.

What I want you to do is flip your thinking. Let's start with the INSiGHT System. They have no idea how much those are worth. When I bought my first system, I positioned that technology to create authority, celebrity, and expertise. I positioned it as a *value* because they know that technology, anywhere you go in a healthcare office, is going to be very expensive. X-rays? Several hundred dollars. CAT scans? Thousands of dollars. They have no idea where this technology lands.

Back in 1992, I was charging $100 per scan: the initial scan, a scan for every family member, and a scan for every progress evaluation. Some of you are charging $30, $40, and some of you doing it for free. What that does, is decrease the perception of value. It causes them to go back to pain-based care, because you didn't build the perception of value high enough.

3. CHANGE THEIR UNIT OF MEASUREMENT

Here's what I mean by that. When someone comes in to see you, they're comparing all of the unknown to what they do know. They're saying, *$2,500 is a lot of money* but it's your job to increase the perception of value before they object, by showing them what $2,500 really is. Let me give you an example: let's say you're selling someone a care plan that is going to cost $300 a month. Everyone has a perception of what value they're going to get for that $300.

If you lack authority, celebrity, and expertise when you say, *it's really not that much* they're still going to look at it and say, *well, compared to a bottle of Advil® that's a lot of money. I think I'll go back to Massage Envy® and get a massage every week instead.* But if you're saying it's $300 a month and you were able to change their unit of measurement and say, *you know, it's the same cost as a monthly Direct TV® subscription and a latte four to five times a week.*

When you change their unit of measurement and what they compare it to, you increase their perception of value.

4. RE-BRAND THE MESSAGE (AND THE RESULTS)

This one almost goes without saying, but the unfortunate stigma attached to the chiropractic brand is that we're uneducated, we're not authorities, and we're not celebrities. I know it's better than it was in the past, but it's still like that.

People don't know you went to school for eight years. They don't know how smart you are, how much you care, how much you train, and how much you invest to become the best person you can possibly be. They don't know any of that nor do they necessarily need to, but the brand of chiropractic is: *you go to a chiropractor to get your back cracked so you feel better.*

So if you underwent a major rebranding by focusing on pediatrics and family, or on wellness or whatever niche is important to you, it doesn't mean you don't take care of people who are hurt. If you don't get trapped by the simplicity of the pain model, you can automatically attain higher perceived value by rebranding. You become a brand like the Fiji® water bottle, not a brand like Nestlé® and there are people out there who are absolutely shopping for that.

5. PRACTICE THE COMMODITY THEORY (SCARCITY)

I mentioned a bit ago that so many chiropractic "manipulations" (not adjustments) are seen as commodities, because *anyone can do them, right?* When chiropractic becomes a commodity and people can get it anywhere, they say, *oh isn't it kind of like a massage?* As a profession, we've commoditized chiropractic. But it doesn't matter. It matters to the profession, but it doesn't have to matter to you because what you *can* do is practice scarcity. I remember saying this hundreds and hundreds of times until it wasn't true anymore: *I'm the only doctor of chiropractic, I'm the only chiropractor that is invested and utilizes this technology as a centerpiece to his practice in this community, I'm one of the very few chiropractors in the nation that has invested time and substantial money into the resource of having this technology at the forefront of my practice.*

Our Epic Docs can say, *first of all, I want to thank you for finding us and for being here. I'm honored to be one of the very few chiropractors in the world who trains with the number one community of chiropractors who are all focused on helping people like you and your family.*

Scarcity sells. All of the sudden, they don't want to go to someone else that has a better price than you do or more convenient hours than you do, because you have shifted their perception of value. Scarcity doesn't only apply to the obvious things. Look, when I cut my hours from 60 to 17, that was a practice move. That was a perception move. *He's busy. He's only here certain times. He must be really good. The parking lot is full.* The fewer spaces in the parking lot, the more people want what you have. The fewer tables available when you make your reservations, the busier that place is going to be. It's the same everywhere and for every business. Practice the theory of scarcity. Do not be a commodity. Stand out in the crowd.

6. BUILD TRUST BEFORE AND AFTER THE SALE

Another way that's congruent with the first five strategies, is to build trust before and after the sale. How? Social proof. Testimonial stories. Facebook Stories. Facebook messages. Your website. Videos. Audios. Pictures. I mean listen, I know some of you don't love turning on your phone and videoing, or doing Facebook Lives, or thank you videos for every single thing that happens, but this stuff MATTERS.

I had something I called a "Freedom Wall" in my practice, where we would hang up items our patients no longer needed after being in our care. At one point, we even had a wheelchair literally suspended from the ceiling of a hallway... seriously. We had full blown plug-in nebulizer machines (not just inhalers) that people gave up because they didn't need them. We had things like old prescription bottles, along with professional shadowboxes of our patient's stories mounted on the wall. Why? Because it's not just before the sale when you need to build trust, it's after the sale too. When you eliminate people's fears and build their trust, they will place their perceived values in you.

The lower the fear, the higher the perceived value. They are entering your practice with a lot of questions, and a lot of fears: *Is it going to be like it was before? Is it going to work for me? Is it going to be worth the money?* Any time you can build trust through social media, DO it. Don't look at this as something you have to do exclusively on Facebook. Look at this as a trust exercise. You are getting people to trust that you will be there for them, that your team is the best, and that you have trained to be the best. This doesn't have to cost you money, either. This is a strategy you can focus on that's guaranteed to make a radical difference in your business model.

7. COMPARE AND CONTRAST

Compare and contrast is one of my favorite strategies and it's closely related to the third strategy we just discussed: changing their unit of measurement. One way you can dramatically increase perceived value is by comparing and contrasting before you get to the pricing question.

So, what does that look like?

Imagine you're doing a Day 2 and you're about to talk about how long it's going to take to get them well. They're going to compare the value of their freedom, their time, their business and everything else with what you're going to say:

So Tony, if I was your personal trainer and you wanted me to help you get ready to run your first marathon, say it's a Boston Marathon, how long and how often do you think we'd have to train? Tony is going to say, *oh probably every day up to the event day.* To which I would respond, *let's say the event is nine months away, and we train pretty much every day and then taper down a little bit at the end. Why would we do that?* Tony will say, *well, because I'm out of shape and I need it and I don't know how to do it on my own. There's a lot to learn and a body needs to get accommodated right?*

You say, *exactly. The reason we would train daily is because your physiology has to adapt. The muscles, the ligaments, the joints and your neurology all has to adapt and that takes time. You can't go from bench pressing 100 pounds to bench pressing 300 pounds in a couple of days by simply joining the gym and only showing up once or twice correct?*

It's the same thing with chiropractic. But we are so good at what we do, and we're such experts in how we apply our protocols and systems within our practices, that it won't take nearly that long.

In fact, preparing you for lifetime wellness care should only take approximately 4-5 months and we'll only need to see you three times per week until we establish those changes.

If you're working with a Mom, ask her if she or anyone she knows has had braces.

The answer will obviously be yes. When you ask her how long it took to correct the teeth, she will answer *about two or three years.* Dig a little deeper and ask her some more questions: why would it take three years to straighten some teeth? *Well, I don't know, but I guess it's because they've been crooked for a while.* Exactly, and it takes a while for them to move and then it takes even longer to hold them in place. And how much do braces typically cost? *About $3,000.*

Well, here's the good news, it's not going to cost nearly that much nor take nearly that long. In our practice, we have the experience and expertise necessary to ensure that you get the results you desire. As long as you're committed to getting those results, we can get you prepared for lifetime wellness care in (insert YOUR care plan recommendations here) 4-6 months and at a fraction of the cost!

They just got a freakin' deal. Comparing and contrasting is one of the easiest things you can do. There are endless metaphors and analogies you can use, so pick the one that suits the situation best.

8. SHOW TRUE VALUE

This is very important when it comes to actually presenting your care plan. Once you've utilized each of the 7 strategies, it's time to show them true value. It is important that you show them what this process is going to require of them to invest. I'm talking about money here, so let's just say the scenario is 60 visits at $50 each, plus five reevaluations at $150 a piece. I'd say:

This process of healing is $3,750 and will give you the kind of quality care that you need in order to proceed and move forward. But here's the good news. We make our care affordable because we take care of families. We have prepaid discounts and we have monthly plans, etc.

There's a tremendous amount of science and research that shows the value of saying, normally it'd be $58 but today it's $42. Again, there is so much research behind the power of comparing and contrasting two items at the same time.

For example, take a $52 jacket. One tag says, "Regularly $68, now $52" and the other says "$52". The tag that says, "Regularly $68, now $52" will outsell the other almost every single time. Why? Because people want a deal. So, give them a deal! Not by diminishing the value, but by showing them the actual true value. You don't have to be in sales to do it. You just have to say something along the lines of: *here's how much it normally would be, but we strive to make health care affordable for our entire community.*

When you show them the true value of the care they're receiving, they will trust you. Period.

9. PRACTICE DIFFERENTIATION

Do you know how easy it is to raise perceived value by saying you're different from everybody else because everybody else has a fee? When you enter a community, you usually do a little bit of research. You'll do some research and find out that the average cash adjustment is $42. When you find that out you can either say, *I'm going to charge $41 and get everyone to come in because I'm the low-price leader* OR you can differentiate yourself.

Make yourself and your practice stand out instead.

Years ago, when I sold my practice here in San Diego and moved to Idaho, the average chiropractor was charging $32 (this was back in early 90s). I researched around 40 chiropractors and found that the average was $32. By the way, they were all taking insurance. So I went 100% cash at $42 straight out of the box. I raised it as time went on, but I immediately started at $42. Why?

Because I wanted to differentiate myself.

I didn't want to be anything like anybody else. And yes, it happened on a rare occasion (maybe five out of 100) that would come in and say, *well my other chiropractor was only $32,* and I'd say, *with all due respect, there has to be a reason that you're in my office today. Mary sent you here because what we do is that different.*

Differentiate.

It could be anything. *I'm a family wellness pediatric specialist. I'm a neuro-based chiropractor. We care more than anybody else. We have a better team. We train harder.* Whatever it is that you can use to differentiate, use it. It's not that hard.

10. PUT (THEIR) VALUES FIRST

The last and perhaps the most important way to raise perceived value, is to always put their values first. We've talked a lot about what *we* need, but if you're not good at finding out what *they* value, if you believe *right now* that the people who are coming to you value health, you're sorely mistaken. Some do. Most don't. What they value is feeling good. But you don't just quit. You become Epic and say what they value, what they want according to those values, is to feel good. But what they *need* is to BE good.

Write this down. It's not about *feeling* good, it's about *healing* good. It's not about how fast you feel it's how fast you heal. We have a gap to close but we know how to do that. We are experts. I believe that the Epic community, and that I myself have become one of the best in the entire industry at identifying and closing that gap with such congruence, such simplicity and with such authenticity, that it never causes any confrontation with people.

But you have to understand what *they* value first. It's not a right or wrong answer. If they value feeling well, you have to know that and put that value first. Whether they value their golf swing, their ability to sleep well, or if they value being a better mom, you need to figure it out.

Once we strive to *understand* what they truly value and put that value first... now that's the game changer.

16 CARE PLANS

> "DON'T TELL ME HOW MUCH YOU KNOW, SHOW ME HOW MUCH YOU CARE"
>
> -DR. DAVID JACKSON

This book is not about how to create care plans, how to sell care plans or how to get patients on care plans, but I would be remiss to not bring up this crucial part of the communication and conversion process.

Historically speaking, a care plan was created once you understood someone's needs and desires. The current situation for the majority of chiropractors looks something like this: *Mary, after everything you've told me and due to my assessment, we found the problem. I think I can help you. We're gonna get at this a couple of times this week and we'll see how it goes.*

Again, we know how it goes. This lasts about 9 to 12 visits and then the plan goes out your front door never to return. The strategies we've already discussed in Chapters 14 and 15 will radically help influence and change this, but at the same time there are critical components of the *process* of care planning that you must understand. The first of which is, it's called a *care* plan for a reason. The word care is carefully selected. It's not just the care I'm going to give them, but it's a caring plan.

We've got to stop counting their money.

We've got to stop worrying about their money and start worrying about their ability to get their health back. We can't focus so much on if they have a third party or if we think they can afford it. We have to focus on what they *need*. The truth will do. With this in mind, set yourself up to be a hero.

Be the hero by telling them the truth.

Don't underestimate the power of a human being, especially a mom. Don't underestimate how grateful she'll be when you tell her not what she wants to hear, but what she knows she *needs* to hear. She wants to hear that she is okay, or that her child is fine or that it's only going to take one visit. They want to hear, *I can crack your neck and your baby's autism will go away,* but they know they *need* to hear the truth. So tell them the truth. Let them digest that.

So, what is the truth?

It's *your* truth as we discussed in Part 1 of this book. It's *their* truth as described in Part 2. It's combining those two into THE truth as described in Part 3 of this book. Your ability to raise their perceived value and to communicate the truth will result in a care plan that is accepted, at minimum, 85% of the time.

Whether that care plan is three times per week for 36 visits or three times per week for 60 visits or twice a week for 12 visits. You will give them the appropriate care you believe they need. That is what we've got to put forward again.

What I need you to understand is that you are going to have to make assumptions. Now, you know what they say about assumptions, don't make them right? You'll make an ass out of you and me. But I have found that the majority of chiropractors, myself included, make assumptions. Here's what we mostly assume: they're not going to have the money. They're not going to want the care. They're going to want to use insurance if they have it. They won't have the time. They only want to be in here until they get fixed and feel better.

We make assumptions that put us on our proverbial heels.

We sit back in our chairs and assume they don't want what we have. I was there at one point. Let's contrast that to where I am now and where you need to be now. Be on your toes, lean in and make an assumption.

They took time off of work. They found a babysitter. They fueled up the car. They called your office. They filled out your paperwork. They fought their way to your practice. They found a parking space. They put their wallet and credit card in their purse or their pocket and they're sitting in front of you with a problem. They're looking for an answer to the problem and I have the solution. I assume 100% of the time that this person is going to lay face down on my table for the rest of their life.

Am I going to be right all of the time? Nope. Is the chiropractor who assumes they're not going to start, be right all of the time? Nope. I would much rather assume the positive and be wrong once in a while, than assume the negative and be right once in a while. The power of assumption puts you in a powerful mindset: *they want what I have. I'm in charge of this. I'm the expert. I'm the authority. They came to see me.*

They want the truth.

They're tired of everyone's bullcrap. They're tired of people who tell them what they want to hear and only treat the symptoms. They want to get to the actual cause of the problem, and they want their family to be as healthy as humanly possible. They value it and they will exchange that value with me. I'm going to go into the care planning process with that assumption and I'm going to put together the absolute best care plan I possibly can.

I am also going to build the concept of Lifetime Care into that care plan. My communication about their perceived values will help me build a vision of a better life for them. I'm not going to set them up on phase one and then right before their very last visit say, *oh by the way, let me talk to you about the benefits of wellness care.* During care planning, I am going to set a future pace for them. I'm going to communicate *possibility* thinking so they can see something bigger. Most people can't see past their noses. If there's a problem right in front of them, I'm going to move that problem temporarily out of the way and paint a picture of the life I know is possible for them to have once they agree to think long term.

I'm going to *care* when we lay out their plan.

I'm not going to care about how much I will get paid. I'm not going to care about what happens to my patient visit average. I'm not going to care about my patient visits or my collections. Oh I care, but not now. I cared enough to set up a value system, a law of exchange and a belief system that guarantees all of this is going to happen.

The only thing I care about when I create a care plan is getting their results and maintaining my reputation, because those are the only two things that truly matter.

17 BEING EPIC

...IS THIS AS GOOD AS IT GETS?

If I were to go back to those years when I was failing in practice and became an auto mechanic, no one could have possibly convinced me that the life I currently live was going to be mine.

I wouldn't believe that it was possible for anyone in my situation. When I stand where I stand today and I look back upon my life, it's easy for me to see what happened: I'm successful by choice not by chance.

I don't share anything in this book, on a stage, or to the chiropractors I so passionately train and help grow in order to impress them. I do so to impress upon you the potential you have to live an Epic Life of BEing Epic.

When I was young, I grew up as a surfer and a skater in Southern California. My older brother, whom I love, is two years older than me but we've never had (and still don't have) anything in common. He's an engineer and wears a pocket protector. I'm a surfer and almost never wear shoes. We could not be any more different of people from the same mother.

My little brother, Michael, was five years younger than me. He was my best friend in the entire world. I loved him more than anything. I looked after him. I protected him. I taught him everything I knew. We always had fun together. I taught him how to surf and the little shit became a better surfer than I was.

On one particularly cold, crisp morning we went out for Dawn Patrol, i.e when you get up just before the sun rises and you paddle out to get the first waves before anybody else. We hopped in my little red race car with our surfboards balanced precariously in the back and headed down to a break called Salt Creek in Laguna Beach. When we pulled up, the break was going *off*. Six to ten-foot sets, offshore with perfect peeling barrels, a-frames, rights, lefts, and no one was out yet. It was going to be an unbelievable day.

We both paddled out as fast as we possibly could and I caught the first wave and took it all the way to the shore. That would have been enough for my day. I could've called it and said, *thank you Jesus, that was such an amazing day.* But I turned around, hungry to get more and as I scratched my way through a set that had just broken, I came back to the outside to see my little brother getting ready to take a wave, all alone with the sun rising, the wind blowing off the back of the wave.

He paddles and drops into a *perfect* 10-foot left-hander. As he stands up, just about to get into what we call the green room, a barrel tube ride, I look and there he is with this big shit eating grin on his face with three dolphins right next to him, their fins just magically gliding along the face of the wave.

As the wave went by and I ducked underneath and popped out the other side, I had a thought that hit me so deeply, so profoundly: it couldn't get any better than this. **This is Epic.**

That beautiful moment occurred sometime in 1985 and it never left me. A few years later, my little brother was tragically killed by a drunk driver. He was 20 years old. He left me that day but that memory and so many others have never left and never will.

When I decided a decade ago to share my message, successes, struggles, tragedies and triumphs with the chiropractic profession in an attempt to help move them forward and was thinking of a name for my company, that memory became crystal clear in my mind.

It couldn't get any better than this. **This is Epic.**

I knew I found the name in memory of my little brother Michael.

For 30 plus years, I've worked on myself to BE Epic. For over 20 years I've traveled the highways and byways of the profession to help other people BE Epic. For over 10 years I've helped chiropractors to define what that means to them.

What does it mean when I say, BEing Epic? Who are we as a community, as a culture in chiropractic, as the fastest growing, number one most connected and successful group of chiropractors in the world?

We are Epic because we define what it means for ourselves- not for the community and not for others. We understand that building this incredible practice, building an Epic Practice by learning how to communicate the truth and get people to want what they need, is a valid and very important and small thing when it comes to life.

Why?

Because ultimately, my purpose as a chiropractor, father, husband, friend, leader, accountability and mastermind partner, coach, and philanthropist is very different from my purpose as a business. The purpose of my business is simple: to fund my personal life. That's very different from the purpose of why I'm a chiropractor. Very different from the purpose of why I've had an incredible relationship with my wife Nicole for 28 years.

That purpose drives me toward my vision, pushes me and propels me. Part of BEing Epic is having a clearly defined purpose and a community of people where strategies are shared openly and crowdsourced to help me BEcome a better version of that person pushing me towards my purpose.

So, who are we? Who are you to BE Epic?

You are the chiropractor that draws a line in the sand and says, *mediocrity is not for me and I will not tolerate it in my life. I won't allow someone to write my story for me. I take the pen and I take control. I take charge. I build a life that I desire and deserve based upon my service to humanity.*

Looking back on my journey is humbling and exciting. I've won big and I've lost big, but I wouldn't change any of it. Through a process of BEcoming Epic, I've focused not only on who I need to be now and not just what I need to DO, but who I need to BE in order to get what I have in this world.

And I don't mean just stuff. I'm not a "stuff" guy. I mean experiences, impact and influence. Legacy. Who do I have to BEcome?

That's who we are. That's who I am and that's who you must decide to BEcome. If we can help you BEcome that, I'd be honored. My team would be honored. What we focus on, what we do is help each other BEcome Epic. Epic Practice is not about David Jackson… it's about YOU.

We have a full team of Docs in the trenches, bent over a table every single day just like you and they are crushing it. Every one of them started where you are right now. They started with an idea and a hope. They started with a word, an ember of passion. They wanted **more**. Each one of the chiropractors who make up Team Epic have massively successful family practices, nearly all of them making seven figures and beyond in 100% cash environments with little stress and more time they can spend with their families. They have associates who are valued parts of the team and are paid very well, a far cry from most out there who "eat our young".

In Epic we help support each other in our journeys. We share strategies and train as a group and individuals weekly. We come together and train on a quarterly basis and roll up our sleeves to BEcome better both at practice and in life. We have all the content and resources any DC will ever need. We hold you accountable to your success. We have small Velocity Accountability Groups that meet together. We train your staff and we help shepherd their growth process.

Epic is not about me. It's about people exactly like you who started out as clients who saw 100 patients a week. People who were stuck, maybe just like you, but were committed to something bigger than themselves. They were committed to being held accountable. Committed to a process. Committed to a journey that took them to places at the time they didn't think were possible but now they're here. Now they're on the inside helping other people do the same thing.

We have this crazy idea that paying it forward is not just a fun, trite statement, but that there's meaning in that. Who we are, who you are, what we do to BE Epic and how we get it done- that's for us to determine. It's for me to determine the life that I want to build, that they want to build, that a client seeks to build. And yes, having an Epic Practice is critically important... but not at the expense of an Epic relationship or BEing an Epic parent or having Epic freedom. Or having an Epic bottom line and actually being massively profitable, paying down your debts and having financial freedom just by doing the one thing you can do better than anybody else.

BEing Epic is a process, it's not an event.

BEing Epic is connecting to a vision that scares the hell out of you.

BEing Epic is having a purpose that pushes you toward a vision while the vision simultaneously and in perfect alignment, pulls you toward something bigger.

BEing Epic is having big goals and being held accountable to those goals along the way, so you know you're heading in the right direction.

BEing Epic is having values that act as the guardrails so when you accelerate around the corners of life and you lose traction, you don't go off the edge.

BEing Epic means you're not going it alone. You've got coaches and people that can show you the way, save you hundreds of thousands of dollars of mistakes. I call it ignorance tax because some people have made it ahead of you. Learn from them, learn from us.

I wrote this book because communication is one of the 9 essential gears required to build your Epic Practice which in turn contributes to your Epic Life. As I said, it's an important one, second only to mindset, but none of the gears are optional. They're all critical.

It's why we developed Epic Accelerator, our success training system that gives you the Truth, Tools and Results you deserve.

Right now, as you read these final words in this book there's a little girl within three miles of your office who is suffering. She's not well. She may have chronic ear infections that have led her to the pediatrician on multiple occasions. They may have suggested tube surgery. She's been on multiple rounds of antibiotics and had an anaphylactic reaction. She's been hospitalized more than once.

Maybe it's a little boy, two miles from your practice who at four years old has just been diagnosed with Sensory Processing Disorder and his mother only wants one thing: she wants her son to look her in the eye and say, *I love you mom* but he just can't.

Why is BEing Epic important? Because it's our responsibility. To be competent. To be connected. To be trained. To be resourced. To be accountable. To be capable to communicate value and get those kids and their families face down on our tables so we can unlock that which interferes with their God given potential.

That's our responsibility. That's what it means to be Epic and if I, or we, can help you further along in your journey to BEcome more than you've ever believed you could be, to achieve an impact at a greater level than you ever thought was possible for your community and your own family, join us. BE Epic.

At the end of the day, the truth will hurt. Or, at the end of the day, the truth will set you free.

What I do know is that always, the Truth Will Do.

RESOURCES

You know now that the truth will do... now it's time to implement and take action! Visit myepicpractice.com to find out more about Epic training programs and discover additional resources to help you master the essentials needed to build a foundation that success can and *will* be laid upon!

Live demonstrations: myepicpractice.com/truth

Website: myepicpractice.com

Facebook: facebook.com/EpicPractice

Email: support@epicpractice.com

THANK YOU

I've been asked what drives me by more than a few people over the years. Impact is my source, my fuel and creating it is my purpose... a purpose that I do not do alone.

I am the man I am today BEcause of my beautiful wife Nicole- Thank you for BEing the force that drives me to BEcome the best that I can BE- always. I love you more than words can describe and am committed to living out our Epic Love Affair, forever and a day.

To my youngest daughter, Taylor- Thank you for always showing me what it truly means to push through and fight for what matters in life… even when it's hard. You inspire me beyond words and fill me with pride. I love you profoundly.

To my middle daughter, Blakely- Your pursuit of BEing you and knowing exactly who that is provides me with a joy and sense of awe that is as rare as you are. Thank you for BEing the very meaning of authentic and for reminding me to dance to my own drum. I love you soooooo much.

To my oldest daughter, Morgan- At 6 years old, you said to me, *Daddy, I love words* and your passion to follow that love has brought us closer than my limited vocabulary can express. I'm a profoundly better human BEcause I have had the honor of BEing your Daddy Man as you develop into the badass woman you are. To say "I love you" somehow falls short but I rest in knowing that you know I Love You!!!

...**And as my publisher, yes, my badass daughter Morgan-** You know my intentions, desires and hunger for creating Impact in this world and your tireless efforts on behalf of your publishing company Epic Impact Press are the very reason this book exists... Thank you.

To Jeffrey Stamp, PhD (x2)- You've been my pocket scientist, trusted advisor and best of friends for over 15 years. Thank you for your wisdom, support, experiences, and for BEing "Uncle Stamp" to the girls.

To Dr. Tony Ebel- You are like a brother to me and meeting you just five years ago was a gift that has allowed us to save countless lives together. Thank you for always BEing so damn Epic!

To Dr. Jake Grinaker- You've been Epic since the day I met you. Watching you BEcome the man and leader you are today inspires me to new levels each and every day. I am in awe of your talents, drive and capabilities and together we are Epic BEcause of you.

To Dr. Jeff May- You trusted me in the beginning. As the very first Epic Practice client, it is a pure gift to have watched you grow from a young wide-eyed DC to running one of the most successful practices in the world. Your growth as a business owner, leader, and father pushes me to always BE more.

To Dr. Patrick Gentempo- Thank you for seeing beneath the surface and pushing me to greatness.

To Reggie Gold- Thank you for BEing the clarion voice of truth and teaching me and countless others how to BE congruent within it.

To the many pioneers who paved the way- Thank you for your ultimate sacrifices and lessons on what it means to BE Epic.

To my brother Michael- Thank you for showing me how to truly live and to BE Epic during the short time you were in my life. I love you and miss you bro.

To my Mom- Thank you for showing me how to overcome, teaching me to never quit and for instilling within me the values that I have shared in this book. You taught me how to BE honest, how to care and how to speak the truth. I love you.

MEET THE AUTHOR

DR. DAVID JACKSON

Dr. David Jackson is a chiropractor, speaker, entrepreneur and success coach who has impacted tens of thousands of people with his simple yet profound principles of Truth and Success.

Known throughout the chiropractic profession as a passionate purveyor of truth, Dr. David has been called the best communicator of our day and his ability to teach authentic approaches custom-fit to an individual doctor is ɪnparalleled.

ʼing risen from the ashes of failing nine times in his first ɿnd a half years of practice, he has parlayed the learned into several world-class family cash and businesses, including what is now Epic ʰe profession's first and most effective online urce.

Over the last 30 years, Dr. David has helped over 4,000 chiropractors create and build their dream practices without all the hype, BS, and high cost prevalent in the profession today.

Driven by innovation and a proven track record, Epic ensures doctors are supported, empowered, and equipped with the Truth, Tools, and Results they need to finally create the practice of their dreams and most importantly, create the life they *deserve*.

Dr. David has a 28 year Epic Love Affair with his incredible wife, Nicole and is 'Daddy Man' to his three girls, Morgan, 26, Blakely, 22, and Taylor, 21. Nicole and his daughters act as his personal 'why' who drive him to BE Epic.

PORTFOLIO

THE TRUTH WILL DO

HOW TO GROW YOUR CHIROPRACTIC PRACTICE BY GETTING PATIENTS TO WANT WHAT THEY NEED

BY DR. DAVID JACKSON

ISBN: 978-0-692-10356-2

PUBLISHED BY EPIC IMPACT PRESS

PUBLISHER & EDITOR-IN-CHIEF: MORGAN JACKSON
LINE & CONTENT EDITOR: MEGHAN ELLIOTT
COVER ART: PRAHARI MAHARDIKA